Jim Wilson's
Container Gardening

Container

TAYLOR TRADE PUBLISHING

Jim Wilson's
Gardening

Designed by Barbara Werden

Published by Taylor Publishing Company
1550 West Mockingbird Lane
Dallas, Texas 75235
www.taylorpub.com

All photos, except as noted, are by the author.

Library of Congress Cataloging-in-Publication Data

Wilson, James W. (James Wesley), 1925–
   Jim Wilson's container gardening / Wilson.
      p.   cm.
   Includes bibliographical references.
   ISBN 0-87833-190-5 (pbk.)
      1. Container gardening. I. Title:
      Container gardening.

SB418.W529 2000
635.9'86—dc21   00-042593

10 9 8 7 6 5 4 3 2 1

Printed in the United States of America

To my grandchildren,

Kathryn Amanda, Jeff, Adam, Anna,

Devin, and Drew.

May they grow into gardeners.

Contents

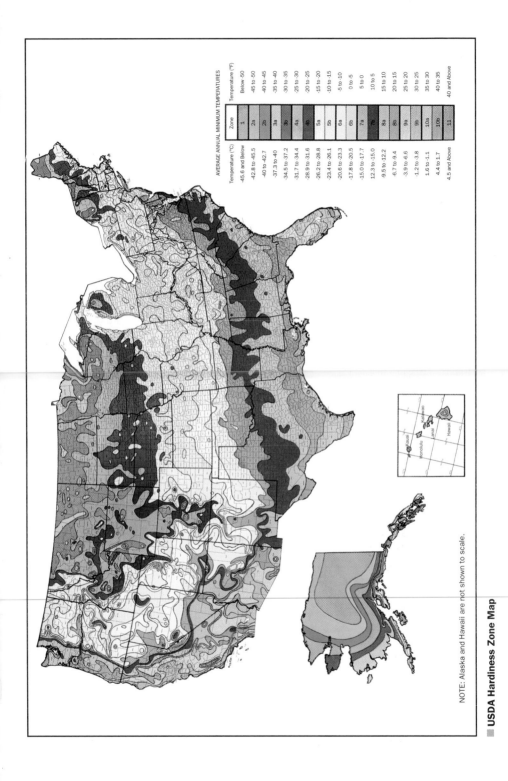

AVERAGE ANNUAL MINIMUM TEMPERATURES

Temperature (°C)	Zone	Temperature (°F)
-45.6 and Below	1	Below 50
-42.8 to -45.5	2a	-45 to 50
-40 to -42.7	2b	-40 to -45
-37.3 to -40	3a	-35 to -40
-34.5 to -37.2	3b	-30 to -35
-31.7 to -34.4	4a	-25 to -30
-28.9 to -31.6	4b	-20 to -25
-26.2 to -28.8	5a	-15 to -20
-23.4 to -26.1	5b	-10 to -15
-20.6 to -23.3	6a	-5 to -10
-17.8 to -20.5	6b	0 to -5
-15.0 to -17.7	7a	5 to 0
-12.3 to -15.0	7b	10 to 5
-9.5 to -12.2	8a	15 to 10
-6.7 to -9.4	8b	20 to 15
-3.9 to -6.6	9a	25 to 20
-1.2 to -3.8	9b	30 to 25
1.6 to -1.1	10a	35 to 30
4.4 to 1.7	10b	40 to 35
4.5 and Above	11	40 and Above

NOTE: Alaska and Hawaii are not shown to scale.

USDA Hardiness Zone Map

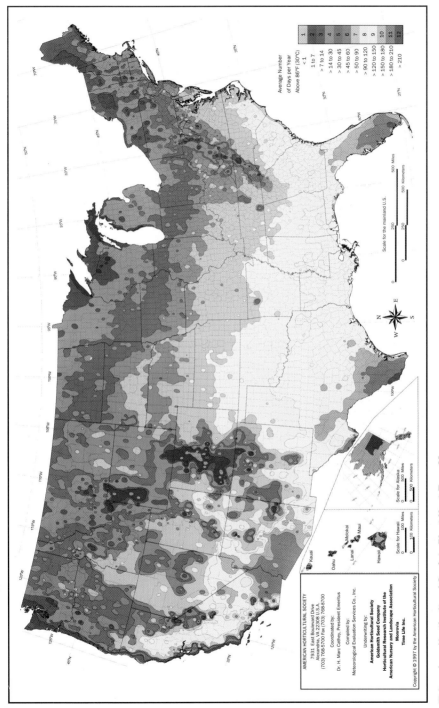

Average Number
of Days per Year
Above 86°F (30°C)

1	<1
2	1 to 7
3	>7 to 14
4	>14 to 30
5	>30 to 45
6	>45 to 60
7	>50 to 90
8	>90 to 120
9	>120 to 150
10	>150 to 180
11	>180 to 210
12	>210

Scale for the mainland U.S.

0   250   500 Miles

0   250   500 Kilometers

N
W   E
S

AMERICAN HORTICULTURAL SOCIETY
7931 East Boulevard Drive
Alexandria, VA 22308 U.S.A.
(703) 768-5700/Fax (703) 768-8700

Coordinated by:
Dr. H. Marc Cathey, President Emeritus

Compiled by:
Meteorological Evaluation Services Co., Inc.

Underwritten by:
American Horticultural Society
Goldsmith Seed Company
Horticultural Research Institute of the
American Nursery and Landscape Association
Monrovia
Time Life Inc.

Kauai
Oahu   Molokai
Lanai   Maui
Hawaii

Scale for Hawaii
0   100 Miles
0   100 Kilometers

Scale for Alaska
0   500 Miles
0   500 Kilometers

American Horticultural Society Plant Heat-Zone Map

Jim Wilson's
Container Gardening

Introduction

Everybody's Doing It!

I'd better qualify that headline. Let's make it nearly every gardener in North America. However you state it, during the past two or three decades, growing ornamentals, herbs, and food crops in containers of manufactured soil has evolved from a mere blip on the gardening radar screen into a major revolution. So who or what is fomenting this revolution? Must we use manmade soil and grow in containers? Isn't the topsoil in our gardens sufficient?

There's no move afoot to turn gardeners away from things natural. And yes, fertile garden soil is perfectly good for growing ornamentals and food crops if you leave it where Nature put it. But garden soil doesn't behave well when confined to containers. You will like the performance of manufactured nursery mixes (call them potting soils if you wish) much better.

Actually, the revolution in containers

came about through the happy confluence of several developments in manufactured soil, containers, advanced cultivars of plants, and lifestyles. It has culminated in some of the most beautiful container plantings imaginable! As I travel this country and abroad lecturing on gardening, I am seeing more and more plants I consider outstanding in all respects.

I like these creative containers of ornamentals so much that I am doing everything I can to interest more gardeners into trying their hand in planting their own. Cheerleader, pusher, puller, enthusiastic advocate, enabler . . . you name it, I've been doing it for several years . . . whatever it takes to introduce gardeners to growing plants in containers outdoors. I could see the new containers, new plants, new potting soils, new fertilizers, and new ways of combining them coming through the pipeline, and it got me all worked up. Everything in this book has resulted from an interchange of information at my lectures or impressions picked up

■ (opposite page) Palm fiber "teepee" holds pots of anthurium, *Phalaenopsis* orchid, and ivy.

■ (top) *Begonia* 'Dragon Wing' in a large, oval
tub. Grow this cultivar in partial shade with
protection from wind; it tends to be brittle.

■ (bottom) *Geranium* 'Fantasia Flamingo',
Acorus gramineus 'Ogon', false licorice
(*Helichrysum petiolare* 'Moonlight'), and *Lantana*
'Pink Caprice'.

during photographic expeditions. And I
can tell you one thing for sure—gardeners are no longer willing to settle for the
ordinary. They are already moving toward the outstanding and the extraordinary in plants and containers.

But why should you as a hobby gardener aspire to growing anything other
than everyday plants in standard clay
pots? Candidly, the mass-produced, pre-
planted dish or basin gardens and hanging baskets on sale at garden outlets can
look surprisingly good, if not great.
Some are quite imaginative. So, for
starters, go ahead and buy one or more
of them. Or, buy a single plant that you
especially like and grow it in a container—just to get started in this new
style of gardening. On the other hand, if
you are looking for a rationale to invest
time and money in planting your own
personalized containers, think of it as
nurturing your own creative growth.
(But don't say it aloud; it would be a sure
way to get a funny look from anyone
nearby!)

True, in sizable towns you can visit
the shops of talented garden designers or
nursery growers and find one-of-a-kind
planted containers that would make your
garden the talk of the neighborhood. If
you succumb to the temptation and buy
one, set it in a heavy box in the back of

your SUV or station wagon and drive home at a sedate pace. Take the turns slowly; such creations are somewhat fragile. They can be expensive, not only because of the creative time and materials that go into them, but also because they need to have been grown for a while in the nursery to give them that "settled-in" look. Whatever you do, don't load planted containers or plants in an open pickup truck or convertible and speed homeward. The blasting wind will tousle, wither, and scorch the plants enroute.

I see growing ornamentals, herbs, and vegetables in containers outdoors as the ultimate creative exercise. In assembling the components for highly individualistic container plantings, you will have to call on your appreciation of all the aspects of art: color, texture, sculptural forms, even the motion of plants in the wind, and visitations by butterflies and hummingbirds. When you put all your talents in play in selecting the combinations of plants and containers that are most appealing to you, you will find your skills will sharpen from year to year. You will move on to larger, more beautiful containers, displayed and combined artistically, and planted with new, rare, or novel cultivars. You can treat them like living furniture that can be moved from

■ **An exquisite urn at Fearrington Resort, North Carolina, shows off a purple palate of Persian shield, tricolor sweet potato, and trailing torenia.**

place to place, grouped together or spread out, until you find just the right site and elevation to display them. In gardening, the means to the end can be much more fun than the end itself.

Earlier I mentioned changes in lifestyles as a force in the container plant revolution. However, lifestyles won't stand still long enough for me to describe how they affect container plantings. Certain trends are predictable: smaller yards, longer commutes, less time for gardening, and a keener appreciation of plants as an artistic medium. For the

latter we can thank more and better gardening programs on TV, better gardening books and magazines, Saturday morning radio garden programs, great botanical gardens, Master Gardening training, and access to the information superhighway. Together, these changes have made container gardening an additional outlet for gardening urges rather than a replacement for gardening in the ground.

In the chapters that follow, I shall deal in depth with the container gardening revolution and the newest in containers, manufactured soil, plant cultivars, and maintenance of plantings. I only hope that the virtual reality of PC monitors, the Internet, and the flickering face of television will not lure us away from a healthy involvement with gardening and landscaping. Somehow, despite our reliance on things electronic, we should recognize that we need the renewal of our spirits that only plants and their creative uses can bring. Even when we move on to an apartment or condo, and say goodbye to our trees, shrubs, and flower borders, we still need that renewal. If you begin gardening in containers now, you can continue in your new landless digs, on a balcony, terrace, or patio. Just a few plants will suffice to sustain your spirits.

One

How Did Growing in Containers Get Started?

Wealthy gardeners have been growing plants in containers for thousands of years. But not until a revolution took place in commercial greenhouse and nursery production of flowers and woody plants did gardening in containers become standard practice among home gardeners across North America. The development of manmade or manufactured potting soils for use by commercial growers of greenhouse crops and nursery stock made the difference. Such potting soils have been given a variety of names, including "artificial soil" and "soilless media," so named because the premium grades contain no real soil. This technology has made it possible for home gardeners to grow ornamentals and food crops in containers much more successfully than with garden soil or garden soil amended with compost.

Thank You, Commercial Growers!

Without the manufactured soils that evolved for producing nursery stock in containers, growing ornamentals and food crops in pots, tubs, and troughs would still be the province of a few advanced gardeners. Instead, it is now one of the fastest-growing segments of home horticulture. I watched the development of manmade potting soils almost from its beginning. Some of the first "nursery mixes" developed on the West Coast consisted of composted coarse redwood sawdust (plentiful at the time), with just enough coarse sand for weight to keep pots from blowing over. Optional additives consisted of Canadian sphagnum peat moss as a source of "fines" for sequestering water and nutrients, limestone, and a phosphate source to assist in root formation. Manmade potting soil was an idea whose time had come, because digging rootballs in tree and shrub production fields and wrapping them in burlap for handling was removing top-soil at an alarming rate. Also, plants grown in containers of manufactured soil grew at a predictable rate and suffered less from waterlogging and the root rots associated with it.

Peat Moss and Pine Bark or Fir Bark

Western nurserymen wasted no time in adopting manufactured potting soils because with them, they could grow better plants quicker and on less ground. Shortly thereafter, southern nurserymen jumped on the wagon, after research proved that their locally plentiful pine bark, when properly aged and graded, made an excellent base for nursery mixes. They, too, used peat moss as a source of fines, but added more limestone and phosphate to their mixes, except when growing azaleas and other acid-loving species. Growers in other areas began to use ground (pulverized) fir or alder bark as a base for nursery mixes. In general, the bark of hardwood trees proved to be less desirable for potting soils than that of the needle-leafed conifers because its fibrous texture made it difficult to incorporate into mixtures. (That fibrous nature, however, makes shredded hardwood bark very good for mulching around plants in landscapes.)

Peatlite Mixes

At about the same time, research resulted in a different sort of potting soil, the "Cornell Mixes" or "Peatlite Mixes" developed at Cornell and other agricultural universities. These soils were designed for growing bedding plants and potted plants in greenhouses, and are fine-textured as compared to soils manufactured for growing nursery stock in containers outdoors. Some of the Cornell Mixes are composed of peat moss and Vermiculite (heat-expanded mica) plus a trace of starter fertilizer and limestone. Others contain some finely ground pine bark as well, and perhaps Perlite (heat-expanded silica) in addition to Vermiculite. This information is relevant to home gardeners because many of the "potting soils" sold in plastic bags in garden centers are formulated like Peatlite Mixes and are too fine-textured and slow-draining to perform well in large containers outdoors.

Sawdust

Typical sawdust from sawmills is seldom used in manufacturing soils because it tends to decompose rapidly, causing the remaining mixture to settle and become more dense, which leads to waterlog-

■ **Part of the selection of containers at MacDonald's Nursery, Virginia Beach, Virginia.**

ging. However, home gardeners, after thorough composting, can combine sawdust and shavings with pulverized pine bark in homemade potting soil mixtures. Sawdust from wood treated with preservatives should not be used.

And Did Containers Change!

I can remember when, as a young seedsman, I called on greenhouses when they were growing bedding plants in wooden "flats" of topsoil modified with compost and peat moss. When a customer wanted to buy plants, a worker would block out however many were needed, as you would divide a sheet cake for serving. Larger plants were sold in clay pots. When clay pots were re-used, the workers scrubbed them with diluted bleach. On pot-washing days, the workers were not happy campers.

When producers of woody nursery stock began to shift from growing in the ground to growing in containers, they first used metal pots shaped much like their clay predecessors. Metal pots held up well in shipping, but were difficult to deal with at garden centers. Before taking plants home, the customer would

■ (top) Large, fragrant sprays of old-fashioned heliotrope in the author's garden. The modern dwarf varieties remain compact when planted in containers.

■ (middle) One of the many forms of plectranthus in Dr. William Holloway's garden in Greenwood, South Carolina, shows how a single plant can make a display in a sizeable container.

■ (bottom) The white variety of drought-resistant narrow-leafed zinnia, *A. angustifolia*, is one of the best flowers for containers that can't be watered frequently.

have metal pots split down the sides with a special tool. When ready to plant, the gardener would bend the sides of the split pot apart to make the rootball pop out. You could get a nasty cut from the sheared metal, and the containers couldn't be re-used. It didn't take long for nursery growers to switch to plastic pots for most plants. At first, plastic pots were quite thick, but with improved technology, they could be made thinner while retaining rigidity and strength. Technology also made possible the use of thin plastic for small pots and market packs for bedding plants.

The drab color and texture of commercial nursery containers aren't pleasing to most home gardeners. For landscaping, they want containers that are not only durable and utilitarian, but attractive as well. Thus, as growers began to swing over from growing in the ground to container culture, the selection of containers especially designed for landscaping burgeoned. Retail garden centers now devote large areas of floor space to attractive clay pots and faux terracotta PVC pots, basins, and tubs, wooden planter boxes, concrete and composite containers, wire hanging baskets and half-baskets, strawberry jars, urns . . . whatever your heart could desire. Displays of plant stands are just as diverse.

Expect, also, to see lightweight hypertufa (HY-per-TOO-fah) containers appearing in garden centers. Gardeners like the durability of concrete containers but not their extremely heavy weight. Hypertufa combines the resistance of concrete to freezing and thawing with the light weight of peat moss, vermiculite, or perlite, along with the rapid acquisition of a patina of algae, moss, and eventually, lichen.

An Avalanche of New Plants

For centuries, ornamentals were improved mostly by selection and increase of desirable plants. Hybridization of zinnias, marigolds, fibrous-rooted begonias, and petunias had just begun when World War II interrupted its progress. Now, seed companies are using sophisticated techniques to speed up the production and evaluation of experimental hybrids. And a new avenue of plant improvement has opened up—the entry of plant producers into plant breeding. Old companies such as Ecke, once known mostly for their cultivars of poinsettias, now are searching the world for promising new species of ornamentals for growing in pots and larger containers. They, along with relatively new companies such as Euro-American Propagators, are joining established American plant producers such as Ball in West Chicago, Illinois, in a drive to change the face of ornamentals. Seed breeders such as Goldsmith, Ball Seeds, Bodger, and Waller (names you seldom see in home horticulture because they are wholesale growers) are using advanced genetic procedures to speed up plant improvement. The Americans are running hard and fast because competitors in Asia and Europe are right on their heels, if not leading the race. This rush toward plant improvement means for you more colorful cultivars, resistant to weather stresses and diseases. Resistance to insect damage will come, but more slowly, as will the restoration of fragrance to flowers.

Gardeners, Fasten Your Seat Belts! (Then Relax)

You can shout at the top of your voice, "Stop the world, I want to get off!" but the makeover of gardens, plants, seeds, containers, fertilizers, and gardening how-to will not only continue, but accelerate. Grab the passing train early and hoist yourself aboard, or you'll find yourself running to catch up. Once aboard, you can relax and enjoy the benefits brought about by scientific advancement. After all, gardens serve as our

■ Clay frog planted with variegated ivy 'Goldheart' and variegated bugleweed (*Ajuga* sp. 'Rainbow').

sanctuaries from stress, as reservoirs of serenity, as links to other life forms, but they can't work their magic if you feel so rushed that you are compelled to organize every minute of every day. Slow down, decompress, look around (really look, don't just glance), and enjoy a benevolent environment made more beautiful by the seed and plant industry, with your help.

Two

Containers

Only a decade or two ago, you might have found a limited assortment of rather small clay pots and a few cachepots in a few garden centers, and virtually none in others. (Cachepots are designed for indoor use and have no drainage holes.) But the times are changing! In all developed countries, and especially in North America, you can now find a rich assortment of sizes and types of containers, some of awesome dimensions. Many are so beautiful in their own right that they could be positioned in the garden and not planted, but rather used as objets d'art.

I am delighted by the new bounty of containers, for I love to browse displays for new colors, shapes, and designs. Now that containers are flowing in from foreign manufacturers, prices have fallen and sales displays have grown. Two kinds of the newer container designs intrigue me. One in particular is the rough-textured, blackish-brown clay pots and urns from Mexico. Some of them are adorned with lifelike iguanas in bas relief. The other kind is the blonde, heat-tempered, sometimes embossed or incised clay pots from Texas and Italy. They are fired at such a high temperature that they ring like a bell when tapped with a coin. Common Mexican clay pots give off a dull "thunk," like a ripe melon. Both kinds are vulnerable to damage from freezing and thawing, but gardeners soon learn to dump their contents at the end of the growing season and store them indoors.

If you are a browser like me, you probably have a favorite place or two where you shop for containers and adapted plants. One of my sources, Craven Pottery at Commerce, Georgia, is about an hour from my home, down the interstate. They make some of their pots from native red clay and import others from various regions of the world. Some of Craven's pots are so large that you can stand in them and barely peek over the rim! While there, I ramble through their sales yard, packed with fountains, statuary, wrought-iron creations, plant stands, and trellises, and enjoy their planted containers.

■ The highly popular earth-toned containers from Mexico.

Purchasing Containers

Rather than giving a checklist for use
when buying containers, let me offer
some general guidelines:

Drainage Holes

All containers for outdoor use need
drainage holes and perform better without saucers. You might think that water
trapped in saucers would prolong the
time between waterings, and you'd be
right. The problem with saucers is that
during rainy periods, water stands for
some time in them and keeps oxygen
from reaching the bottom layer of soil in
the pot. Root tips begin to die, and roots
can rot.

Container Size

For fast-growing ornamentals, start
with containers of 5- to 10-gallon or
greater capacity. Smaller pots dry out too
quickly, and plants grown in small pots
quickly become potbound. For shrubs
and other large ornamentals, and for vigorous vegetables, start with containers of
20- to 30-gallon capacity.

Container Shape

You may be familiar with the standard height-to-width ratio of "standard" pots. In addition, you can buy "squat pots"; short, broad basins; and pots shaped like bells. Although standard pots drain a bit faster than squat pots and basins, base your choice mainly on the mature height (or foliage canopy size) of the plant or combination of plants you intend to grow in it. The most pleasing ratio of top growth to container capacity is two to one. Your pot needs to be tall enough so that the plant when mature doesn't look top-heavy. This ratio is easier to visualize with free-standing containers than with hanging baskets.

Clay or Plastic?

Now you are getting into aesthetics vs. economics. Clay pots are more handsome than "faux terra-cotta" pots of PVC, but are heavier, cost more, and are more likely to break. The best clay pots ring when struck with the edge of a coin. (If you hear a vibration, check the pot closely; it may be cracked.) Bargain-priced clay pots are usually fired at lower temperatures and tend to be soft and fragile, even when coated inside with asphalt to reduce water absorption. In arid climates, gardeners usually opt for plastic containers because they hold water a bit longer than clay. I lean toward the beautiful glazed clay pots from Malaysia and Thailand, mostly, I suppose, because cobalt blue and teal look so good against green foliage.

Special-Purpose Pots

These include strawberry jars, tall jardinieres or urns, half-baskets for hanging on walls, wire baskets with handles for twining topiary, and shallow saucers for growing small spring bulbs, cacti, and succulents. Don't try to economize by buying small hanging baskets; you will soon regret it.

Wooden Boxes

Planter boxes and window boxes come in many sizes, most of which are, unfortunately, too small for growing flowers through the season. Planter boxes and window boxes should measure 10 to 12 inches front to back, at least 12 inches high, and long enough end to end to either span a window sill or to look in proportion with its other dimensions. Don't waste your money on small, narrow, planter boxes; they dry out too quickly.

Western redcedar, eastern redcedar heartwood, cypress, redwood, black locust, or willow are some of the relatively rot-resistant woods that are used for making planter boxes, buckets, and tubs. (You won't find the two latter woods in a lumber yard.) If yellow or white pine, fir, or spruce is used, it should be primed and painted inside and out to inhibit water absorption and subsequent rotting. Occasionally, you will find planter boxes made of treated wood. The preservative won't harm plants and it should prolong the life of the box over several seasons. Treated wood, once it has weathered a bit, can be painted with a stain, but paint doesn't want to stick to it. I wouldn't plant a food crop in a container of treated wood without shrouding the inside with plastic.

Drainage holes of 3/4-inch diameter should be drilled every 6 to 8 inches. The life of a planter box can be prolonged by lining it with plastic, stapling the plastic in place, and punching drainage holes in it. Use galvanized, coated, or aluminum deck nails or screws in construction. Box nails will lose their grip from expansion and contraction, and they will rust quickly. When you mount a planter box on a window, be sure that the drainage water does not run down the side of the house, but drains on the ground.

Concrete Containers

If concrete weren't so formidably heavy and industrial looking, it would be the material of choice for containers. Blends of Portland cement and sand are used for making containers, but no gravel (unless the surface is meant to be brushed to expose the pebbly aggregate). Concrete pots are usually sold in highway outlets that also sell benches, tables, and plant stands along with assortments of concrete ducks, bunnies, turtles and frogs, gnomes, and birdbaths, as well as fiberglass deer and whatever else suits one's fancy. Their weight notwithstanding, choose large concrete containers over small ones. Small containers dry out too rapidly. Look your purchases over carefully; try to avoid concrete with bubbles, soft spots, or knicked rims or corners.

Bags of Potting Soil

Some greenhouse growers of tomatoes plant seedlings in openings cut into 2-cubic-foot or larger, plastic bags of potting soil laid flat on the greenhouse floor. Before positioning a bag, they tip it up and punch a few drainage holes in the bottom surface. It isn't beautiful, but it is easy to do, and it works. You could do the same with a bag of potting soil laid on a concrete bench, and planted

■ Troughs and tubs of various sizes and shapes are used to grow Don Sudbury's collection of alpine and rock garden plants, many native to the mountains of Utah.

with trailing flowers to cover the bag. Clever manufacturers have adapted this idea to make 1-gallon plastic pouches that are filled with potting soil. The bags have strap handles so they can be hung on fences or walls and planted with small kinds of flowers such as pansies or lobelia, or with herbs.

Hypertufa Troughs, Sinks, and Pots

These lightweight containers are made of Portland cement blended with peat moss and perlite or vermiculite instead of sand, strengthened with Fiber-Mesh and, optionally, with acrylic hardener. Originally, they were created to emulate the fast-disappearing Scottish or English watering troughs or sinks chis-

eled from solid blocks of sandstone. Hypertufa containers can be textured for aesthetic appeal, and after aging will take on a patina of algae and moss. Hypertufa containers can be left outdoors in hardiness zone 5 and south, but where winters are quite severe, they can gradually erode from freezing and thawing.

A few specialists are making hypertufa troughs, pots, and sinks for sale, but so much hand labor is involved that they are expensive compared to concrete containers. Consequently, many home gardeners who have the muscles necessary for hefting bags of Portland cement are making their own hypertufa containers, mostly in the shape of traditional rectangular troughs and sinks. Hypertufa containers are well worth the time, effort, and expense that goes into making them, but you need to follow "recipes" and procedures worked out by trial and error. See Chapter 8 for detailed instructions.

Pots, Pans, Buckets, Tubs, Retired Work Boots, Apple Crates, Fish Boxes, Rusted-Out Wheelbarrows, etc. etc.

If you can drill or punch drainage holes in it, or line it with plastic and punch drainage holes, you can fill it with potting soil and grow plants in it. And why not? Having fun is what gardening is all about, and if it outrages the sensibilities of a few fastidious neighbors, let 'em gossip. The important considerations are: did your plants grow well, and did you enjoy them? Enough said.

Valuable Kettles and Carts

Don't drill drainage holes in antique kettles, carts, or other devices used to hold pots. Instead, lay bricks inside and set liner pots on them. Every week or two, empty the collected water from the bottom of the kettle or cart and set the plant back in it. You don't want to have water standing for long; it could go sour or breed mosquitos.

Winter Care of Containers

Gardeners in USDA hardiness zones 7 and north should plan to empty and store all except concrete and hypertufa containers in a garage or shed during the winter. Freezing and thawing can cause clay pots to slough off exterior layers or to crack. Wooden containers suffer as badly, because freezing and thawing can loosen nailed joints and can even loosen barrel hoops. As a precaution against carrying over root-rot organisms from year to year, swab the inside of used clay or concrete pots with a 10 percent solution of bleach. Let it soak in for a few minutes before rinsing.

Overwintering Perennials

When you empty containers for winter storage, you can "heel in" hardy perennials to carry them over the winter. To do this, dump out the container on a flowerbed and retrieve any perennials. Dig a trench, lay the root systems in it, and pull soil over them. Water the plants thoroughly and mulch around them so they can develop anchoring roots before the soil freezes. They can be dug up and replanted in a container the following spring.

■ Due to transportation costs, containers are expensive in New Zealand, and fixtures such as porcelain sinks are often pressed into use for growing rock garden or alpine plants.

Three

Soilless Mixtures

Shopping for Manufactured Soils

I have watched home gardeners as they shopped for potting soils, soil conditioners, or mulches, and my heart has gone out to them. Many producers of soilless mixtures have so complicated their product lines that consumers find it difficult to make rational decisions at garden centers. And a few manufacturers, sad to say, are so obsessed with the bottom line that they are formulating mixtures from the cheapest available raw materials. This obsession causes them to book business with stores that place profits ahead of consumer satisfaction. In this chapter I will tell you how to recognize high-quality soilless mixtures and how to avoid mixtures that may look good but produce poor to mediocre results.

Mixtures for Filling Pots and Larger Containers

When it comes to soils for filling containers, home gardeners need only two major formulations:

Potting soil: a rather fine-textured, moderately slow-draining mixture for filling small pots for growing plants indoors. These are formulated like the Cornell or Peatlite mixes mentioned previously.

Container mix: a coarser-textured, moderately fast-draining mixture for filling larger containers for growing plants outdoors, or for backfilling when setting out plants.

Mind you, this stripped-down list does not apply to commercial growers, where a slight modification in a manufactured soil may improve the growth of a given species. When you are growing hundreds of thousands of plants, even a minuscule improvement in each plant can improve overall profits significantly.

A Plethora of Packages

There is justification for mixes blended especially for terrestrial orchids, for cacti and succulents, African violets, and for bonsai, all of which prefer customized soils, and for a near-sterile mixture for

gel flower is one of the best filler flowers for containers, as it weaves its spikes of purple, blue, pink, or white oms among more substantial flowers.

starting seeds and cuttings. But manufacturers are reaching when they package special mixes for many different kinds of plants of other species. They would be hard-pressed to show any difference in performance between their special mixes and all-purpose, high-quality potting soils or container mixes. The plethora of packages is based more on the desire for more exposure for their brands on store shelves than on demonstrable differences in plant performance.

Reach for High-Grade Mixes

The highest-grade **indoor potting soils** for home gardeners are made from premium-quality Canadian sphagnum peat moss alone, or mixed with a little aged ground pine or fir bark for slightly faster drainage. Vermiculite can be added for increased water retention, or perlite can be added for faster drainage. A trace of starter fertilizer may be added, and just enough limestone to increase the soil pH to a level preferred by most plant species. The highest-grade potting soils are fortified with controlled-release fertilizer for all-season feeding.

In the South and West, the highest-grade **container mixes for outdoor plants** are made principally from finely ground pine or fir bark with enough peat moss to fill the need for "fines" (fine materials) to sequester moisture and nutrients. Heavier amounts of starter fertilizer and limestone are incorporated to meet the needs of larger, more vigorous plant species. Some premium-grade nursery mixes contain slow-release forms of fertilizers, and perhaps some absorbent to help extend the time between waterings. A bit of nontoxic wetting agent may be added to help rather dry nursery mixes take up water faster. In the North and Midwest, where freight charges on southern pine bark are high, coarse peat moss or less expensive organic amendments may take the place of pine bark in manufactured soils. This results in mixtures that are somewhat heavier and slower to drain than those formulated for the South and West. Gardeners in those areas have learned to adjust their watering schedules accordingly. It also means that when purchasing container soils in the North and Midwest, gardeners should be careful to avoid the very heavy mixes that will drain too slowly for optimum growth of plants. Such ultra-heavy mixes are often cheapened with sand or water, neither of which are useful in mixes.

■ Custom-planted basins of cacti and succulents appeal to customers at "Big Jim's" Garden Center near New Plymouth in New Zealand. These species can get by with occasional watering.

Absorbents

Small packages of potting soils and container mixes may contain an absorbent polymer that helps them to retain more water. The granular absorbent imbibes water and releases it to plant roots after water held between soil particles is exhausted. In general, absorbents are worth their extra cost in dry, windy climates or in nursery mixes used in hanging baskets, which tend to dry out rapidly.

Potting Soil Semantics

Most manufactured soils are labeled "potting soils" even though their formulations may make them more suitable for growing plants in large containers outdoors. Your best approach is to read the information on the back of the packages to gather as much as you can from it. Even better, find the nursery manager or a senior employee of a garden center or builders' supply store and ask him or her which mixes they use for growing their own crops in small pots or larger containers. They will probably point you toward stacks of 3-cubic-foot or larger bags, which deliver more value per unit than small packages.

Organic Soil Conditioners

Organic soil conditioners are used for breaking up clay soils and for helping sandy soils hold water and nutrients. They are coarser than potting soils or container mixes, and can be made from many kinds of by-products such as sawmill waste, cottonseed or peanut waste, dried cattle manure, stable litter, rice hulls composted with chicken manure, or from yard waste composted with sewage sludge. Peat moss is a good soil conditioner that requires little processing other than harvesting and drying, and removal of sticks and leaves. Organic soil conditioners are designed to be mixed with soil in the garden to make it easier to work, to enliven it through increased microbiological activity, and to allow it to absorb water faster while improving drainage. When landscaping, I would never have "topsoil" hauled in. Rather, I would buy a soil conditioner to improve what is already there. "Topsoil" is the original "pig in a poke."

Organic Mulches

Organic mulches are coarser in texture than soil conditioners and are designed to be spread over the surface of the soil to conserve moisture, discourage weeds from sprouting, and gradually improve the soil as it decomposes. Neither soil conditioners nor mulches can completely replace fertilizers. Their content of major plant nutrients is so low that they aren't subject to fertilizer laws requiring plant nutrient analyses to appear on packages. The major benefits of organic mulches are gained from physical or biological, not chemical processes. Organic mulches decompose rather slowly in the North, but rapidly in the South and Southwest due to higher temperatures and longer summers. Tunneling by earthworms also removes some of the decomposing interface between mulches and the soil. The busy little wigglers take particles of organic matter down into their tunnels and, in the process, gradually improve the texture and structure of the soil.

My Favorite Soil Conditioners and Mulches

My favorite organic soil conditioners are made from composted pine bark, and my favorite mulches are made from either pine bark or hardwood bark. In parts of the West, the more plentiful fir bark is often substituted for pine bark and is equally effective. I like the way the bark mulches look and the benefits they bring to garden soil. On mulches I draw the line only on the ones made from chipped wood and waste wood such as discarded pallets. The chips tend to float away in heavy rain, decompose very slowly and lead to nitrogen drawdown in the soil. Even when dyed with artificial color, they still look like chipped wood.

What to Avoid When Purchasing Soilless Mixes

Some mixtures, regardless of what name they are given, contain materials that serve few functions other than to de-crease their cost to the manufacturer. "Topsoil" (and the term can cover a multitude of sins) is occasionally added, but can contain weed seeds and, God forbid, herbicide residues. Poor quality "muck," which is a kind of peat composed of decomposed wood, sedges, and other aquatic growth, looks black and fertile, but is another offender. It can contain high levels of mineral salts and weed seeds, and tends to become soggy. Cattle manure can be very alkaline and loaded with viable weed seeds, unless heat-sterilized. Mushroom compost, while it makes a barely passable soil conditioner, is partially spent peat moss or composted straw and manure, which without additional composting has poor physical characteristics for potting soils or container mixes.

The worst offenders in manufactured soils may be fine sand and excessive water. There is no justification for adding either to potting soils. Fine sand impedes drainage rather than improving it, and excessive water makes mixtures heavy and difficult to carry. All I can figure is that it must cost more to dry out wet materials than the extra freight costs they cause. Novices might see the heavy mixes as a better buy than mixes that contain just enough water to make them easy to wet. Not so, of course.

And sand . . . it adds nothing to mixes other than weight and is justified only for areas that are windy, where containers might blow over, or for plants that require the extra-fast drainage provided by coarse, graded sand or granite meal. It is sad that in this corner of a peaceful business like gardening, the old axiom "let the buyer beware" rules the marketplace.

Don't be fooled into believing that the most visible brands of potting soils and nursery mixes in stores are of the highest quality. Often, the space given a certain brand on shelves is determined by how much the manufacturer will pay the retailer to stock his brand. Again, trust the nursery manager or a senior employee of a builders' supply chain. Ask them which brands they use when potting up house plants, roses, or nursery stock, and follow suit.

Making Your Own Potting Soils and Nursery Mixes

Some gardeners who plant several large containers each year make up their own mixes for potting house plants or outdoor ornamentals and vegetables. They make up sizable batches and keep them clean in closed garbage cans or plastic lug boxes. Mixing soils can be a dusty process, and you should wear a mask.

Wash out a wheelbarrow, fill it halfway with ingredients and mix them with a clean hoe.

Ingredients for an All-Purpose Potting Soil for Indoor Plants

Two parts high-quality Canadian sphagnum peat moss, by volume. Buy it by the bale or large bag for best value.

One part ground pine bark soil conditioner rubbed and sifted through 1/2-inch hardware cloth.

One-half part horticultural Perlite or Vermiculite.

One heaping tablespoon of pelleted dolomitic limestone per gallon of mix.

If you are thinking about using straight organic soil conditioner or an organic mulch to economize, keep in mind that the soil conditioner may contain "topsoil" with weed seeds and plant disease organisms. Some mulches are graded into coarse chunks. Chunks are useless in mixtures. Don't add any fertilizer; it is difficult to distribute evenly throughout the mixture. Don't overdo the mixing, as too much agitation can break down the peat moss. Add just a little moisture from a sprinkling can as you are mixing. Shovel the mixture into the storage can and make more batches until the can is full.

■ Square hypertufa container planted with variegated obedient plant (*Physostegia* sp.).

Ingredients for an All-Purpose Mix for Outdoor Container Plants

Two parts ground pine or fir bark soil conditioner. It doesn't have to be sifted.

One part high-quality Canadian sphagnum peat moss.

One heaping tablespoon pelleted dolomitic limestone per gallon of mix.

One heaping tablespoon gypsum per gallon of mix for additional calcium and sulfur.

You won't need to add limestone if you live an area with very hard water—indeed, it may be impossible to find limestone in western garden centers. Follow the directions given above for mixing. If you blend in controlled-release fertilizer, don't moisten the mix, as water can initiate the release of nutrients and a buildup of salts in the mix. It is safer to add controlled release fertilizers when filling containers for planting.

Note: Homemade mixes, and packaged mixes as well, may show a weblike growth after a few weeks of storage. It tends to bind particles together in clumps. The growth simply tells you that the natural process of composting is continuing, and this process can in no way harm you or your plants. Simply crumble any aggregations to restore uniform texture to the mixture.

Variations on Homemade Container Mixes for Growing Vegetables

You can make up to as much as one-half of the mixture from inexpensive materials such as composted sawdust, leaf mold, or mushroom compost. As much as one-quarter of the mixture can be dried cow manure. All of these materials decompose more rapidly than ground bark or peat moss, and you may have to add a topping to containers of vegetables in midseason. I would not add garden compost to container mixes for growing vegetables, as it could inoculate the mix with plant disease organisms. When growing fruiting vegetables such as tomatoes, peppers, and squash in containers, you must add dolomitic limestone to the soilless mix to prevent plants from developing blossom-end rot, a symptom of calcium and magnesium deficiency, usually worsened by drought.

Keep the Lid on Tight

Much of the value of manufactured soils over garden soils is their virtual freedom from soil-borne diseases. When not in

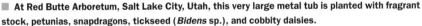
■ At Red Butte Arboretum, Salt Lake City, Utah, this very large metal tub is planted with fragrant stock, petunias, snapdragons, tickseed (*Bidens* sp.), and cobbity daisies.

use, keep the lids on containers used for storing soil mixes to exclude dust, and store the scoop inside the sealed container. Even when you are filling containers periodically from a large plastic bag of potting soil, it's a good idea to store the opened bag in a lidded garbage can, especially seed starter mixes.

Reusing Manufactured Soils

I can empathize with the many thrifty gardeners who want to save and reuse manufactured soils, but I wouldn't do it. Soils go through many physical and chemical changes during a season of supporting plant growth. Most impor-

■ Three plants of white pentas fill a 10-gallon container and billow gracefully over the rim.

tantly, a high percentage of the fine materials in the original mix decompose to humus, then oxidize and disappear, leaving a coarse mix that drains too rapidly. Also, mineral salts tend to build up, and certain major and minor nutrients are either depleted or accumulated in undesirable amounts. Root-rot organisms may have gained a foothold. In short, you are better off dumping spent soils atop flower beds where they can serve as a mulch, or be turned under as a soil conditioner. You can also add spent soils to your compost heap.

If you feel compelled to reuse mixes, add one-quarter to one-half by volume, fresh, moistened sphagnum peat moss and, except in the arid West, one heaping tablespoon of pelleted dolomitic limestone per gallon of reconstituted mix. If you fertilize with liquid plant food, make sure it contains micronutrients to replace those depleted during the previous season.

Stand by Your Man

When you find a brand of potting soil or nursery mix that works for you, year after year, stick with it. Formulating horticultural soil mixes is a demanding business, requiring a tight program of quality control without letup, and no relaxation of standards, despite pressure from retailers for lower prices. I've stuck with one premium brand for more than fifteen years, using it in commercial greenhouses, for landscaping, and to fill containers around my home, and it has never let me down. In today's market, you can't say that about many products.

■ **A display of very unusual container plants in choice containers at Heronswood Nursery includes sedges, rushes (*Juncus*), and plants trained to bonsai form.**

Four

Plants for Containers

Ready to plant your containers? Grab a shopping cart or a red wagon at your favorite garden center and begin choosing whichever plants suit your fancy? Well, yes and no. Sure, you can pick up a few geranium or petunia plants, or impatiens if your site is shaded, and stick them in a 12-inch pot, but let's first stop and think about the opportunity rather than the challenge. Ornamentals don't achieve outstanding status on eye-appeal alone; they need to be suited to your climate, to the season, to the site where you intend to display the container, but most of all, to your particular taste in flowers and foliage. They should retain color for a long period of time, and they should be relatively pest-free and capable of recovering after occasional periods of neglect. That's a lot to remember when you are shopping, so the best idea is to make out a preliminary list from this book and pick and choose from it.

Combining Flowering and Foliage Plants in Containers

You can grow a single kind of a big, vigorous annual, perennial, or shrub in a container and it will look pretty good. Case in point: at this writing I am enjoying a 10-gallon container planted with three seedlings of a bright pink, star cluster flower, *Pentas lanceolata*. They have spread to cover the top of the container and are billowing out over the sides, while growing to about 30 inches in height. Additional plants of a different species in this pot would be too much. Yet, there is much to recommend tasteful combinations of various kinds of flowers in large, individual containers. Here's a checklist to assist you in choosing compatible cultivars.

Sun-Shade Compatibility, and Compensating for Strong, Drying Winds

When you plant more than one kind in a container, all should be either shade tolerant or sun tolerant. Shade plants

■ Container made of tabby (consolidated seashells) and planted with cyclamen for early spring color, at Cloisters, Sea Island, Georgia.

■ Verdigris finish fiberglass container sets off this topiary heart of ivy and trailing wishbone flower (*Torenia fournieri*). The wax-leafed begonias will soon expand to pack the container tightly with color.

might wilt in the afternoon sun, and sun-loving plants might stretch and fail to bloom in the shade. However, many of the kinds that must have shade in the South or warm West will grow just fine in full sun in the North and coastal Northwest if given adequate water.

Many gardens in the Southwest, the Intermountain area, and the Great Plains are frequently subjected to strong, drying winds. Winds can be so strong and persistent that medium-to-tall flowers may be difficult to grow in flower beds, much less in containers. It behooves gardeners in these areas to construct low walls or baffled fences, or to look around for a place that will give their plants shelter. You would be amazed at how much better plants will grow in the lee of a shelter, and how shelter can reduce the frequency of watering.

Mature Size of Plants

Look on the tag. If it doesn't give an approximate mature height, ask your dealer. Choose kinds whose "cube" (bulk) of foliage at maturity will be no more than two to three times the capacity of the container. For example, if a plant grows to 2 feet in height and 1 foot across, its top growth will total 2 cubic feet. One cubic foot will fill a 7-gallon container, thus a container of 5–7 gallons should be in scale with the mature plant. This formula works best for individual plants grown as specimens, but when you plant more than one kind in a container, you can use the cube of the combined top growth for your calculations. Much guessing is involved until you have grown all the cultivars through one season and can easily visualize their mature size. Don't lose any sleep over this one; shears and pinching can keep the top growth in bounds.

Combining Various Habits of Growth

When working with containers, you can generalize that ornamentals will assume one of three forms at maturity: trailing, mounding, or erect. In large containers, you can combine concentric rings of trailing and mounding plant forms, and one or more tall, erect plants in the center for height. The mounding plants can come out to the rim in one or two places instead of being restricted to an inner circle. You can use a single tall foliage plant in the center, or group three slender, flowering plants. Fountainlike plants of spike *Dracaena marginata,* New Zealand flax (*Phormium tenax*), or fountain grass (*Pennisetum* sp.) are often centered in containers to create the dimension of height. Colorful, erect plants of

■ Bas-relief clay pot holds a shrubby copperleaf plant (*Acalypha wilkesiana*) and asparagus fern.

cordyline make good central plants for containers of shade-tolerant kinds.

Creating Pleasing Combinations of Colors and Textures

Generally, it is better to combine either warm colors or pastel colors in a given container, but not both. If you mix the two palettes, also include some plants with gray or silver foliage to reduce the contrast. Plants with blue or white flowers are also good at preventing visual clashes between strongly contrasting colors.

Much has been written about avoiding too-strong contrasts in the texture of foliage, but I think the writers are being too fussy. There really is no substitute for setting the young plants side by side while at the garden center to see how they look together. In container plantings, ferny-leaved plants serve as fillers between plants with bolder foliage. You might find yourself challenged in trying to find a foil for the dominant foliage of ornamental sweet potatoes, but common sense will tell you to bridge the gap between bold leaves and filler plants with species that have medium-sized leaves. A single large container can accommodate a variety of foliage and blossom sizes and shapes. Furthermore, it will look better than one filled will all large-leafed plants

or with little plants with leaves like the ears of mice or grains of rice.

Estimating the Number of Plants You Will Need for a Large Container

The simplest way to estimate the number of plants of each kind you will need is to choose your container first, then select three kinds of trailing plants, one or two kinds of mounded plants, and one erect kind. While at the garden center, find an unused tabletop and lay out your plants to fit the size and shape of the container. Young plants should occupy about 1/2 to 2/3 of the total soil surface area. Leave the balance open for plants to spread or bush out as they develop.

Shall I Go with Perennials or Annuals?

The answer depends on where you live. In USDA hardiness zone 5 and north, keeping perennials alive in containers through the winter is difficult, unless you sink the container to the rim in the soil. There are exceptions. In snowy, mountainous areas and other places where snow covers the ground much of the winter, hardy perennials and alpine species can survive for years in containers outdoors. But over much of the

One of the attractions of gazing balls is their ability to reflect their surroundings. Depending on the angle of view, you can see reflected in this ball ivy, dracaena, geraniums, and variegated plectranthus.

An ornamental banana, *Musa* sp. 'Blood', with false licorice (*Helichrysum petiolare* 'Moonlight').

northern half of the USA, where snow cover is sparse or intermittent, either true annual flowers or tender perennials grown as annuals dominate container plantings.

In hardiness zone 6 and south, consider including hardy perennials in plantings made in concrete or hypertufa containers—pots, troughs, or basins that won't be destroyed by freezing and thawing. Perennials for containers are usually species with small, precocious

plants that will bloom the first season. These are somewhat larger than the wee alpines, but sturdy and free flowering. By including hardy perennials, you can vastly expand your palette of flower and foliage colors, textures, and forms, especially among the shade-tolerant species.

One of the most exciting developments in recent years is the widespread marketing of tender perennials from the tropics, Australia, New Zealand, South Africa, the Caribbean, and Southeast

Asia. Even in Minnesota, you will see plants of lantana, pentas, tropical verbenas, and mandevilla for sale, along with Dahlberg daisies, cobbity daises, gerberas, and so on. They are sold at bud or bloom stage, usually in larger containers than seed-grown bedding plants. But where they really excel is in the warm West, the Northwest (away from the cool coast), and in zone 7 and south in the southern USA.

Seed-grown annuals haven't stood still. Seed breeders are putting larger flowers on shorter plants, making them more heat resistant, and infusing such vigor that the plants remain in good color and condition through the dog days of summer. I was reminded of their success when in late August heat, I stood admiring the trials of wax-leafed begonias at Park Seeds, just down the road from my farm. There they were, row on row, flourishing in full sun, looking as if someone had groomed each plant just prior to my arrival. And this had been the hottest summer on record!

Using Herbs in Combination with Ornamental Vegetables

Some of my favorite container plantings are of herbs alone or herbs combined with ornamental vegetables. Strawberry jars of 5-gallon and more capacity and large basins are best suited to growing assortments of herbs or herbs plus vegetables. The herbs that mature at rather small sizes are best, of course, but you can keep large plants from overgrowing containers by pruning them severely. The choice of truly ornamental vegetables that stay in condition for several weeks is limited but worth trying. Plant mixed colors of Swiss chard, curled parsley, golden beets, peanuts, lovage, and leaf celery with flowers or with herbs.

Don't Forget the Bulbs! (The same goes for corms, rhizomes, tubers, and bulbils.)

Choose concrete or hypertufa containers for plantings of spring-flowering bulbs in October or November. In mild winter areas, they can be left outdoors, but where winters are severe, you should set planted containers inside a garage or other unheated structure. Move them outside when the worst winter weather is over. Lay a screen of chicken wire over containers to keep squirrels or chipmunks from digging up bulbs. They won't eat narcissus bulbs, but can unearth them while digging for edible species.

A horticulturist with the zoo in

■ (top) Hanging basket of false licorice, *Coreopsis grandiflora,* and pink star cluster flower.

(bottom) It would be hard to find a more impressive container than this one planted with the native American beach wormwood (*Artemisia stellarana* 'Silver Brocade').

Denver told me that they routinely plant spring-flowering bulbs just before winter, in concrete containers. They plunge the containers into the soil so that the rim is about an inch below the soil surface, and mulch over them with 2 inches of bark mulch. Apparently, the earth's heat radiates through the container and the potting soil to keep it just warm enough to prevent the bulbs from freezing. Denver, being a mile high, enjoys snow cover during much of the winter, which helps to protect bulbs and perennials. You may have discovered the trick of setting seedling plants of early-blooming annual flowers among spring bulbs when they begin emerging. They will give the planting a beautiful layered effect.

Of the summer-flowering bulbs, callas are probably the best suited to containers, along with agapanthus in mild winter areas. Cannas are good, too, but the foliage is so bold that you have to take care in siting the container and in selecting compatible companion flowers. Caladiums from corms are a favorite shade plant

Now, are you ready to choose the particular cultivars that appeal to you? Well, you might want to take another moment to consider matching flowers to the season. Here's what I mean. . . .

Plants for Summer Color

The assortment of plants for summer color is immense. But when you boil it down to just the kinds that will bloom all summer long from spring planting, the list shrinks. When you narrow it further to just the kinds that will remain compact and not overgrow the container, the list will include less than a quarter of its original qualifying cultivators.

Some of my favorite trailing plants are false licorice (*Helichrysum petiolare*) in both the gray and golden foliage colors and little-leafed forms, variegated vinca vine, sweet potatoes with purple, chartreuse, or tricolor foliage; the lavender-flowered fan flower or scaevola, and the little-leafed, white-flowered bacopa. For hot summer areas the new perennial verbenas, variegated plectranthus like the one called "Cuban Oregano," trailing petunias and Million Bells (*Calibrachoa*) are rapidly catching on. The bacopas look good, but need more water than the others to stay in good condition.

Among the mounding plants, I like the lobelias for cool summer areas. They come in purple and blue, pink, and white. Wax-leafed begonias and the dainty Signet or Gem marigolds will withstand more heat than the lobelias, as

will the silver or gray dusty millers, the silvery-white curry plant, and the tiny but sturdy nierembergia, 'Mont Blanc.' The dainty but durable Dahlberg daisies (*Thymophylla tenuiloba*) make good filler plants among more massive annuals.

Erect plants that won't overgrow or flop are hard to come by. I like the blue mealycup *Salvia farinacea* 'Victoria,' the Madagascar dragon tree (*Dracaena marginata*), or New Zealand flax (*Phormium tenax*) for their grasslike foliage. For large containers with room for erect but bulky plants, try the red-leafed beefsteak plant (*Perilla frutescens*), and the candle or wheat forms of celosia. Where summers are cool, tall snapdragons are a natural for the centers of containers.

Plants for Winter Color in Mild Winter Areas

Trying to keep anything alive in containers outdoors during the winter in USDA hardiness zones 3 through 6 can be an exercise in futility. Hardiness zone 7 will allow a few tough species to survive and set flowers in containers. Pansies, violas, *Primula veris,* white perennial candytuft, along with camellias in protected corners are among the survivors. The hellebores are among the most reliable performers but are touchy about

▨ (top) Variegated agave. These can grow to great size, and their sharp points should be pruned off to avoid injury.

▨ (bottom) Planting pockets can be chipped out of picturesque pieces of driftwood to convert them to planters.

■ Clay pots of dwarfed hydrangeas, with deep pink sweet alyssum for fragrance.

transplanting and don't like to be disturbed.

Matters improve considerably in hardiness zones 8 and 9; several temperate climate species will bloom there during the winter and early spring. They are species that can stand up to the rain and fluctuating temperatures that come from November through February. A short list would include pansies and violas, calendulas, snapdragons, primulas of various species, stock, wallflower, Siberian wallflower, narcissus, camellias, low-growing heathers, and certain of the tree heaths. None of the annuals will survive summer heat and are usually grown just for winter color. After the winter is past, they are interplanted with summer flowers to hide their fading foliage. Heathers, heaths, and the tiny alpine and rock garden plants are grown mostly in cool summer areas such as coastal Central and Southern California, at relatively high elevations in the Rockies, and in alpine greenhouses in northern areas where winter snow cover is sparse.

Utilize Autumn for Color

Garden centers in hardiness zones 8 and 9 offer an extraordinary array of colorful ornamentals for sale during autumn months, including quick-blooming summer flowers such as marigolds and traditional fall flowers such as chrysanthemums, fall asters, and dianthus. You might wish to pull out your exhausted summer flowers and replace them with young, vigorous plants that will give you color during most of the winter. A surprising array of summer flowers can live through mild winters in zone 8 and south: petunias, snapdragons, wax-leafed begonias, heliotrope, marigolds, and verbena, for example. However, these tenacious survivors can't be counted on for more than sporadic color during the winter.

Winter Color in Very Mild Climates

Gardeners in low-elevation California areas, South Texas, protected Gulf Coast microclimates, and North Florida down through Key West can choose from many ornamentals that can bloom right through cool weather, and even withstand a few degrees of frost. South Florida and Hawaiian gardens (USDA hardiness zones 10 and 11) seldom suffer from frost and can support many exotic species in containers through the winter. Bromeliads and spring-flowering orchids such as the cymbidium cultivars are container staples for them. Northern gardeners moving to Florida would be well advised to sign up for a Master Gardening training course to speed up the learning process that they face.

In coastal California where citrus grows without protection (avocados are even more frost sensitive), calendulas, cinerarias, calceolarias, nemesias, sweet peas, fuchsias, and schizanthus are often seen in winter gardens. Inland, where night temperatures are sharper, flowering plants are grown under the protection of eaves, unheated plastic greenhouses, or evergreen trees such as live oaks or California bay. Except for sweet peas, plants for winter color are usually purchased in the early bloom stage and are kept in

■ This gazing ball serves as a conversation piece and reflects the bed of sedum growing in a length of hollow log.

their original containers until the flowers are spent, then sacrificed. Western gardeners visiting the big early-spring flower shows in northern states can only shake their heads in disbelief at novice gardeners being blown away by the big greenhouse-grown displays of calceolarias, cinerarias, and nemesias. Beginners can't wait to buy them, not realizing that such flowers can't stand hot, humid summer weather, even in the unlikely event

the plants survive several weeks indoors until frost danger is past.

Specimen shrubs are often grown year-round in containers in hardiness zones 8, 9, and 10. Citrus, hibiscus, camellias, and dwarf cultivars of oleanders are especially popular, along with evergreen shrubs such as boxwood and myrtle. The worst problem with container plants in these southern zones is rapid drying of the soil during the summer, unless you install automatic drip irrigation. Only "cast iron" plants can endure the heat and dryness between infrequent waterings. The cycads, such as sago palm, and the native coontie or Florida arrowroot are especially popular, as are desert plants such as yucca, aloe, and agave. Cacti or succulent species without spines, glochids, thorns, or sharply pointed dagger leaves are useful in containers. Shrubs or large desert plants in containers are seldom underplanted during the summer, but necklaces of trailing ornamentals can beautify them during the winter when occasional watering will suffice.

Cool-Weather Plants for Regions Where Winters Are Short but Sharp

Many gardeners live in hardiness zones 6 and 7. Pansies and the hellebores (Christmas and Easter roses) are among the few herbaceous ornamentals that will live through the sometimes horrendous cold snaps and ice storms, and bloom during warm spells. Snapdragons are a sometime thing for winter color. Much depends on the largesse of Mother Nature. During some winters she holds back the continental polar air and lavishes warm winter days on gardens in the Midsouth and Upper South.

Gardeners there don't exhale until March has come and gone, and with it the threat of late ice storms and killing frosts. During less-favored winters she lets the blue northers rip through the area. The soil freezes an inch deep and in perpetually shaded areas doesn't thaw until late February.

The legendary southeastern gardener, Elizabeth Lawrence, was enthusiastic about bulbous plants for winter color. Many of the species she championed decades ago have yet to be distributed widely, but she persuaded many a southern gardener to plant hyacinths, Roman hyacinths, crocus, polyanthus and hoop-petticoat narcissus, winter aconite, and snowdrops for color during January and February. These grow well in containers but some species prefer not to be disturbed once they have begun blooming. You might pilfer a Do Not Disturb! doorknob notice from a hotel as a reminder to you, but a better idea is to plant the bulbs in hypertufa containers that won't be damaged by freezing and thawing. Overplant the bulbs with hardy hen and chicks and the smaller species of sedums, and you will have all-season color plus the element of surprise when the bulbs shoot up. Sink a few craggy stones into a container mixture made gritty with fine cracked pea gravel or a heat-expanded slate product called PermaTill, and your succulents and bulbs will thrive in a miniature landscape for many years. (I just looked out my kitchen window and my "surprise lilies," *Lycoris radiata,* had popped up overnight and formed flower buds. They would make a great addition to a hypertufa container.)

Of all the plants for winter color in containers in zones 6 and 7, the winter or early spring flowering shrubs are tops. Witch hazel and flowering quince are favorites but need yearly pruning after blooming to keep them from overgrowing. A bit further south, winter jasmine, camellias, sweet olive, and trellised Carolina jessamine put on a great show. If you are concerned about the possibility of losing a treasured container plant, you can place a layer of pinestraw, Spanish moss, or sphagnum moss in a larger container, set the container-grown plant on it, and stuff around it with more insulation. Sometimes, just setting the container on the ground and banking a little soil around it will bring plants through southern winters with flying colors.

Dwarf cultivars of shrubs with colorful winter berries also make good choices for containers. You can train flowering clematis up through the branches of shrubs to provide early sum-

■ (top) The fern-leafed verbena, *V. tenuisecta,* stays in bounds all summer long, isn't pushy, yet continues to bloom for months on end despite heat and humidity.

■ (bottom) Ornate clay pot with false licorice, dracaena, and fuchsia.

■ See the artistic effect created by grouping high-quality clay pots of various sizes and designs? The tall flowering plant is *Agastache cana,* native to the southern Rockies.

mer color, and can drape trailing summer flowers over the rim of the container.

Pre-Planted Containers

Only a few nurseries in affluent communities offer a large selection of one-of-a-kind planted containers. These retailers usually have a floral designer working for them, a person skilled at combining color and textures, sizes and shapes. Large, distinctive planted containers are rather expensive, but excel as focal points in your garden. Almost as desirable, but not unique, are the production-line basins, baskets, and pots that are planted with pretty much the same sizes and kinds of plants. These products are usually stuffed tight with plants that look great at point of purchase, but soon overgrow the container. They need to be fed often with liquid fertilizers containing micronutrients such as iron. Enjoy them for a few weeks, then dump out the plants and reset them in a larger container filled with fresh mix formulated for outdoor containers.

Now May I Plant? Please?

Your head may be whirling after reading all these considerations. But don't worry; if you heed only a few of the pointers, you should end up with a planted container of which anyone could be proud. Yet, if you are like most gardeners you will want to grow better every year. You will consider ordering and saving choice perennials from specialty catalogs, and perhaps will travel to outstanding garden centers in nearby metro areas to skim the cream from their inventory of containers and plants. By all means, visit your nearest botanical or estate garden yearly. Take along your camera to record the planted containers you especially like. If the plants are not labeled, collar a docent or a Master Gardener volunteer and get the names of the plants.

Be patient during the learning curve. Remember, growing plants in containers is no harder nor easier than growing them in the ground—just different. With a little practice the parts will begin to

■ **Antique dragons at Linden Plantation, Vicksburg, Mississippi, support pots of bronze-leafed wax begonias.**

come together, and you'll find yourself circling one of your creations, murmuring, "Not bad, not bad!"

(For more information on special plants for containers, see Chapter 9.)

Five

The Harmonious Whole

Staging

Now that you have planted a container that pleases you, or one that has obvious potential, what are you going do with it? If it is rather small, you may wish to create two more like it, perhaps with minor variations, and group them at various elevations on plant stands. Stands don't have to be expensive. They can be wooden boxes, concrete benches or tables, lengths of logs sunk into the ground for stability, cement or cinder blocks, stacks of stones, or large pots inverted. Any landscape architect will tell you that there is magic in lifting up objects or plants that deserve special staging. Let me add that staggering the height of odd numbers of containers in a group can heighten the illusion.

Plant Stands

I especially like wrought-iron plant stands—the rustier, the better, although I don't object to a painted-on verdigris finish. But plant stands don't look good plunked down in lawn grass. I like to see them standing on cement or tile squares or flagstones. They look neater, stand straighter, and are easier to trim around. I also like to see planted pots stuffed into antique farm or garden equipment: wheelbarrows, wagons, carts, planters or seeders, big discs from plows, and old wooden boxes. But don't overdo the quaint stuff or you'll have what the British label "an eccentric garden."

Understated Vines

If your yard is small, you may find that lifting containers up to waist or shoulder level tends to overpower your other landscape features. That's when you may wish to plant vines in containers raised on low blocks or feet, and run them up trellises. I wouldn't recommend the big, vigorous vines because they transpire a huge amount of water on dry, windy days. Look instead at the slower-growing vines such as clematis, and the semi-hardy firecracker vines, *Manettia cordifolia* or *M. inflata*. I've grown *M. cordifolia* in

■ Accessories—a faux fruit bowl and a lead lantern—flank a small hypertufa bowl of begonias.

my hardiness zone 7 garden for six years, through winter lows near zero degrees Fahrenheit.

You can buy rustic, diagonally nailed latticework trellises or wrought-iron trellises ranging from elegantly simple to ornate. I would recommend sinking their supports into the ground at the back of the container because attempting to keep them erect and plumb inside containers usually ends in failure.

■ Don Sudbury found just the right setting to display this asymmetrical urn.

The Old Broomstick Trick

But where to place these groups of containers or individual containers of greater size? You will soon tire of lugging them around, searching for just the right site. If you have a sizable yard, try tying flags on sticks cut to the height you intend to stage your creations, and move them around until you like the spacing between them and your vantage point. Don't position any of them further away from a faucet than can be reached by a length of water hose. Leave the sticks in place, and as you can spare the time and money, plant additional containers and replace the flags with them. Call them "landscape focal points" if you will, and you will find yourself seeing them in that light.

No-Brainer Sites

Some sites require no thought. They are predictably attractive—at the point of a peninsula in a shrub bed, around a corner and against dark evergreens for the element of surprise and the contrast of colors, in pairs at the head or foot of stairs, and just off center at the far end of your garden. They ask for you to use them, and you set or hang plants on them . . . walls, corner posts, steep hillocks, stumps, and large pieces of driftwood.

Now for the Test

For years, in my lectures on landscaping with containers, I've asked audiences where containers of vividly colored flowers should be placed—up close to the house or way back in the garden. Most agree with my notion that placing vivid colors out in the far reaches of the garden draws your eye to them and adds apparent depth to your landscape. But I've had landscape architects take the opposite view, and propose siting brightly colored flowers near a kitchen window or patio, and moving the soft pastels to the rear of the garden. So, to avoid a knock-down-drag-out fracas, let's agree to place the various colors wherever we please.

Four-Part Harmony

On one point, everyone agrees. There comes a moment—when your container plants have knitted together and have begun to billow over the rim of your container, and you are giving them their daily drink of water—when you will look around to see if anyone is in earshot and will say something like, "Hey, babies,

■ All the species in the genus *Erigeron* carry the unlovely common name of fleabane, but you couldn't ask for a prettier, more dependable plant than the semi-tropical *E. karvinskianus*. Here it is at an estate in New Zealand, growing in 6-inch pots obscured by the abundant blossoms.

you're looking good! Keep it up!" And when you stop to analyze what it is about your living art that pleases you, you will realize that all the parts are in harmony. The colors of the plants and the container agree. They look good against the background where you have placed them. You have included silvery gray to set off the bright colors. Everything is blooming at once and shows every indication of continuing in color for weeks. The erect plants in the center are standing unsupported, without the aid of a distracting stake. If plants could sing, you wouldn't be hearing the goofy, reedy little elfin voices they are given in cartoons, but a majestic "Gloria" in four-part harmony.

■ (top) Teepee planted with *Thunbergia gibsonii*.

■ (left) Hummingbirds drink from this fountain flanked by large pots of the bush mandevilla 'Red Riding Hood'.

Six

Caring For Plants Growing In Containers Outdoors

The Learning Curve

You can generalize about how certain plants will grow in containers in your garden, but you will not know for sure until you plant and care for each individual variety through a growing season. Certain verities will come into play:

The longer and hotter your growing season, the greater your chances will be of having to replace spent plants of certain varieties. Some plants just can't stand the droughty conditions that are inescapable in late summer, yet some—like vinca vine, Joseph's coat, the tropical shrub jasmines, and *Helenium* 'Loraine Sunshine'—come through dry soil with flying colors.

The longer and hotter your growing season, the greater your chances will be that certain varieties will overgrow and push out less aggressive types. In my containers, *Evolvulus* 'Blue Daze' took over one container, polka-dot plant dominated another, and Petunia 'Misty Lilac Wave' swamped its luckless companions in a large pot. The ornamental sweet potatoes are extremely pushy.

The longer and hotter your growing season, the greater the need to feed often, especially as the season wears on. As plants grow to considerable size, they demand more plant food than juvenile specimens and more frequent irrigation.

The shorter and cooler your growing season, the less your plants will need shade, the less frequently you will need to feed and water them, and the more likely they are to survive and thrive through the entire growing season.

You can do a lot to change the performance of your plants in containers by shifting them up to larger pots when they show signs of becoming rootbound, and by moving them to a location where they will be shaded from the searing afternoon sun. You can also keep root balls cooler and more moist by setting planted pots inside larger pots. Even though the outside pot may feel hot to the touch, the dead air space between the two pots will insulate the inner pot from much of

■ (top) Part of the
Ball Horticultural
trial of sun-tolerant
cultivars in
containers.

■ (right)
Bougainvillea likes
the heat radiated
from this ornate
concrete urn.

the radiated heat. I often plant in recycled black nursery pots and slip them inside slightly larger, more decorative containers.

Water-Soluble Crystalline Fertilizers

The water-soluble crystalline fertilizers can keep container plants flourishing, but they may need to be applied as often as weekly. Each time you water, you flush a certain percentage of plant nutrients out the drainage hole. These little ions are holding on to soil particles for dear life but some have a weaker electrochemical connection and can be washed loose or knocked loose by more active nutrient ions. One major nutrient, nitrogen, also vaporizes as gas. Some nutrient salts accumulate near the soil surface as the water carrying them evaporates. The net result is that, at the most, 20 to 30 percent of the nutrients applied as liquid fertilizers are absorbed by plant roots. And some of that may be "luxury consumption" of nutrients taken up by plant roots, not because they need them, but because they are there for the taking. There is little you can do to increase the efficiency of liquid fertilizers; a certain amount of waste goes with the territory.

Feeding Plants in Containers

Five ways to feed plants in containers:

With water-soluble crystalline *mineral* fertilizers dissolved in water

With concentrated liquid *organic* fertilizers diluted in water

With controlled-release fertilizers mixed with the soil before planting

With dry granular *organic* fertilizers dressed on the surface and watered in

With manure tea of a special kind

We will cover the "how to" before getting into "when" to feed plants. The "why" to feed plants is obvious, as almost everything they receive as rations has to come from you.

Concentrated Liquid "Organic" Fertilizers

The major difference between soluble crystalline fertilizers and concentrated liquid organic fertilizers is philosophical. Both work pretty well, but one is "mineral" and the other is "organic." One can smell like a distant fish factory; the other has no smell, and turns a pretty color when dissolved, along with staining your fingers blue or green. Ironically, if you read the analysis label of the liquid organic concentrate carefully, under "Derived from" you may find that the content of nitrogen and phosphate has been boosted by adding di-ammonium phosphate. This makes the plant nutrient analysis on the label look more attractive but, understandably, turns off purist organic gardeners. Fortified or not, I like to use fish emulsion occasionally because I am convinced that it contains organic compounds that, while they can't be claimed on the label, put a special sheen on plants in containers.

Controlled-Release Fertilizers

Back in the '60s and '70s I worked for a company that manufactured one of the first controlled-release fertilizers. The product worked well then, and still does. It looks like little rounded beads coated with plastic. When you mix it with potting soil, water drives in through the vinyl coating and the little beads swell to twice their original size. Nutrients gradually move into the soil moisture by osmosis and are either trapped by soil particles or taken up by roots. The rate of release of nutrients depends on the temperature of the soil rather than on soil moisture. The warmer the soil, the faster the plant grows, so nutrient release and

plant growth increase at much the same rate. During the past two decades, competing controlled-release fertilizers have come on the market, some with a "complete" analysis (all three major nutrients) and some composed of nitrogen alone. A few are coated with sulfur or wax rather than with plastic.

The duration of nutrient release from controlled-release fertilizers can be partially controlled by the thickness of the plastic coating. Accordingly, you can buy formulations that feed for either three to four months from a single application, or for up to eight to nine months. In short-summer areas the three-to-four-month formulation is the better buy. As a class, controlled-release fertilizers can approach 50 percent efficiency, which is about as high as you can get. They are hard to beat for convenience and for sustained growth and flowering in containers. They always work better when mixed with the soil than when spread on the surface. They should never be mixed with moist potting soils well in advance of use, as the moisture will trigger release of nutrients that will accumulate as salts. When they are mixed with commercial potting soils before they are packaged, the manufacturers are careful to keep moisture below the level that could trigger nutrient release.

Using Both Controlled-Release and Liquid Fertilizers

Some gardeners prefer to supplement controlled-release fertilizers with liquid feeding every two or three weeks. This doesn't require any adjustment of rates. However, if you plan to feed weekly or more often with liquid fertilizer and to mix controlled-release fertilizer in the soil as well, you should apply each at half the rates recommended on the packages.

Dry Granular Organic Fertilizers

Dressing dry organic fertilizer atop the soil in the container and swirling it in is the fourth method of feeding and the least satisfactory. Tankage, blood meal, and cottonseed meal are in this class. Organic fertilizer releases nutrients at a very slow rate when the soil is cool. But when it warms up and microbiological activity zooms, a load of nutrients can be released all at once, especially nitrogen in the form of ammonia. Plant roots near the surface can be fried. Dry granular lawn or garden fertilizers can be just as unpredictable and can cause even more damage. They should never be applied around container plants. Some premium-grade potting soils include garden fertilizers, but they are present in such

An extraordinary strawberry jar imitates the berry itself.

small amounts that they pose no danger to even sensitive plant species.

Manure Tea

The fifth method, manure tea, can only supplement other methods of feeding. It isn't sufficiently concentrated nor bal-

■ Name your color—except black or brown—and you can find it in impatiens. 'Busy Lizzie' is one of the most dependable shade-tolerant flowers for containers.

anced to fill all the nutrient needs of flowering or foliage plants. I have access to a fertilizer with the politically incorrect name of Kricket Krap, and it really is pure cricket manure, a by-product of fish bait farms. When I was raising herbs in greenhouses and they would plateau in growth despite my feeding at maximum safe levels with controlled-release fertilizers, I would drench the potting soil with cricket manure tea. The plants would sit up and whistle. Making the tea is a malodorous process that will not endear one to his or her spouse, but it can bring amazing improvements in growth and color. The gain is worth the pain. The so-called "hot" manures—poultry, sheep, rabbit, and goat—make stronger teas than cattle or horse manure. The fibrous residue left over from making manure tea should be put in the compost heap rather than poured around plants in containers. It can contain distressingly large numbers of weed seeds all primed to grow.

Correcting Deficiencies of Secondary Nutrients

Only the three major plant nutrients are required to be listed on fertilizer analysis labels: nitrogen, phosphate, and potash. Yet, three of the "secondary" nutrients—calcium, magnesium, and sulfur—are also important in feeding programs, especially with potting soils and nursery mixes. Consequently, manufacturers of soil mixes blend in a little dolomitic limestone to supply calcium and magnesium, and rely on either gypsum (calcium sulphate) or the carriers of major nutrient ions to supply the trace of sulfur that plants need. This initial fortification with limestone is sufficient where seasons are short, but where summers are long or where heavy-feeding vegetables are grown in containers, supplementation with limestone and magnesium sources may be required midway through the growing season.

Much guesswork is involved in supplementing feeding programs with additional limestone and magnesium at midseason. In arid areas with hard water, supplementation is rarely necessary, but elsewhere it may improve the condition and color of plants in containers, especially fruiting vegetables. Dolomitic limestone swirled into the top few inches of the soil, at the rate of one heaping tablespoon per gallon of capacity, should be sufficient. It might also help to drench the soil with a solution of Epsom salts (magnesium sulfate) at the rate of one level tablespoon per gallon of water to supply both magnesium and sulfur. Drench the soil with water before applying the Epsom salts solution. Apply monthly.

Micronutrients

Micronutrient deficiencies can usually be avoided by feeding with soluble fertilizers that contain iron, copper, boron, cobalt, zinc, manganese, and perhaps other trace elements. Fish emulsion and seaweed concentrate are good sources of micronutrients. In the West and Southwest, iron deficiencies are common in container-grown plants, caused by iron being immobilized by excessive levels of phosphate and perhaps other salts or chemical bases. Slow-release chelated (extended release) iron is the preferred remedy for iron deficiency chlorosis (severe loss of chlorophyll).

■ Typical assortment of caladiums offered for planting in containers or in the ground, in shaded areas.

Watering

One of the first purchases you should make after planting ornamentals, herbs, or food crops in containers is a water wand. A wand consists of an aluminum tube with an angled end, capped with a sprinkler head that breaks the force of water from a hose. The best models have an on-off lever where the wand attaches to the hose and a flexible joint near the head that can adjust to various angles up to 180 degrees.

The frequency of watering depends not only on the weather, but on the stage of growth of the plants. Common sense or obviously wilting plants will tell you that you will need to water more often during hot, dry, windy weather—usually daily. Mature plants, with a lot of top growth for the size of the pot, or plants with big leaves that transpire a lot of water, may need to be watered twice daily. Don't try to conserve water by trying to eliminate the runoff from the drainage hole. You need to see drainage every time you water. It helps to dissolve and carry away salts that could otherwise accumulate at or near the surface and interfere with root growth.

If you fail to water frequently enough, leaves can turn yellow, develop scorched edges, or, in severe cases, become stressed and drop off the plant. Overwatering is seldom a worry except during rainy, cloudy, cool weather. That's one of the beauties of high-grade potting soils in containers—they drain so rapidly that you don't have to worry about waterlogging. Nevertheless, I like to elevate containers on plant stands, blocks, or those amusing little clay "pot feet" to provide unobstructed drainage.

Many gardeners report that they have trouble with strawberry jars or large urns filled with potting soil. Water tends to wet a narrow cone down through the center of the container without spreading out from side to side, or it will stop partway down the rootball and drain out

■ The growing importance of containers in home horticulture shows in this huge trial of various sizes of pots and plants of hundreds of species and cultivars. Ball Horticultural trials, West Chicago, Illinois.

the planting holes. You can rectify the problem in one of two ways. First, try three drops of mild dishpan detergent per gallon of water in a sprinkling can. Drench a little of the solution on the top, wait a few minutes and drench a little more. If you do it gradually, the detergent will act as a surfactant and will make water wetter. The water will spread out as it dribbles its way down through the soil. Don't use more than the recommended amount of detergent, as a strong solution could harm your plants. Another way is to sink a length of perforated plastic tubing from the top to the bottom of the container. Cap the bottom end before inserting and filling in around it. Fill it full of water or fertilizer

■ Powers Court, south of Dublin, is one of the most popular public gardens in the Republic of Ireland. Petunias in ancient concrete urns flank an earthbound angel.

solution and it will leak out so slowly that lateral transmission of moisture will be improved. Cap the top loosely to keep out trash. You may see roots growing through the holes in the tubing. Don't discourage them; they won't completely clog the holes.

When planting in strawberry jars, especially the type without protruding lips beneath the planting holes, I like to make "gaskets" of moistened, long-fiber sphagnum moss and stuff them in around each plant. The ropy moss keeps soil from washing away from the plant roots and pouring down the sides of the jar. It seals the holes and adds a finished look to the plantings.

A Side Benefit of Watering

When you water your container plants, you can also spray them with a needle-sharp spray of water. It will dislodge many harmful insects or their eggs that otherwise might increase to pestiferous levels. In humid areas of the country, spraying with water is best done in the morning when the sun will dry the foliage. If you water your container plants in the evening, direct the water at the soil and keep it off the foliage, to minimize the danger of foliage diseases. Consider getting a "quick-connect" device for your hose so you can easily plug in a trigger-operated spray in the morning and a water wand in the evening. I have had only modest success with keeping spider mites off boxwood with sharp sprays of water, but the sprays seem to work well with other species of plants.

Automatic Drip Irrigation

Some fortunate gardeners are able to take a few weeks off each summer to travel. Gardens in the ground can usually survive with little or no care until the gardener returns, except in the arid West, where someone should either monitor the sprinkling system or do the necessary watering by hand. But how about containers that need frequent watering? You can set up a drip irrigation system controlled by a timer and it will water as often and for as long as you like while you are away. Such systems are linked to a nearby water faucet, and water is conveyed through spaghetti tubes. Various kinds of emitters are available, including weighted drop-heads for small containers and perforated rings for large pots. With a little tinkering, you can even arrange to feed your plants through the same watering system. Upscale garden centers carry a selection of drip irrigation systems.

Chemically softened water, where

the calcium and magnesium ions that make water "hard" are replaced by sodium, is not good for container-grown plants. It can be used, but more generously than rainwater, so that most of the sodium is flushed out.

Pest and Weed Control

Oh joy! High-quality container soils contain few or no weed seeds. The occasional weed seed may blow in or be dropped by birds, but weedlings can be pulled out of the porous soil with little effort and without disrupting the root system of the star performers. Another joy is the virtual freedom from soil-borne diseases. Both peat moss and ground bark apparently have an antifungal action. They don't protect against plant viruses transmitted by feeding insects, and for that reason you need to investigate biological and botanical methods of pest control, especially for aphids and whiteflies. When you grow only a few plants in containers you may be able to get by with a trigger-operated spray bottle, but most gardeners soon step up to a pump sprayer that can generate a needle-sharp blast not only to distribute the insecticide but also dislodge and wash the little suckers off the plant. An angled spray boom will help you reach underneath leaves to get at concentrations of feeding insects. I rarely use any insecticide, but when I do, it is of the botanical or biological type and targeted surgically to minimize the danger to beneficial or harmless insects.

Bringing Outside Plants Indoors for the Winter

More and more gardeners are growing frost-tender perennials in containers and would like to bring them indoors for the winter. I've been moving tropical hibiscuses, variegated *Ficus benjamina,* and lady palms indoors for a few seasons, to the protection of a cool sunporch. About a month before the first frost, I begin spraying them with insecticidal soap—trunk, twigs, and leaves, above and below. Then, when I move them indoors, they carry few or no spider mites, aphids, mealybugs, cottony-cushion scale, thrips, leaf-hoppers, or their eggs. By springtime, they will have dropped many of their leaves, and will have begun to look ratty, but we enjoy their presence during the winter and accept their temporary decline as unavoidable, considering the dry air indoors and the reduced level of light. On warm winter days we set them outside on the drive and run water through the soil to dissolve and

■ This creeping fig not only hid its topiary form of moss but spread over the square hypertufa container as well.

carry away accumulated salts.

You could handle choice tender perennials in the same way, but not everyone has a sunny porch, nor do they enjoy the short, generally sunny winters of the Southeast where we live. Further north, you would need to move over-wintering plants to the basement and grow them under fluorescent or metal halide lamps. The air in basements is usually cooler and more humid, which makes a better environment for growing plants than the dry, heated air in the upper levels of the house.

Despite "planning ahead" you may find yourself at the coming of the fall season with more plants than you can protect. The beautiful tropical shrubs or vines such as the jasmines, hibiscuses, mandevilla, and allamanda can double in size in a single growing season. That's why during the summer you should root softwood cuttings from your prize plants and carry them through the winter under fluorescent or metal halide lamps. Then, you can either sacrifice your big plants or try to give them to a company that specializes in "interiorscaping." It hurts to see such magnificent plants die from the first killing frost, but when you live north of hardiness zone 9 and don't have a greenhouse or a basement equipped with horticultural lights, that's the way things have to be.

Winter Protection for Hardy Perennials in Containers

Assuming that you are growing plants in containers of concrete or hypertufa that won't be destroyed by freezing and thawing, you can give them considerable protection by simply setting the containers on the ground. That precaution alone should suffice in hardiness zones 7-B and south, but in more northerly areas plants will need further protection. You can bank soil around containers or pile leaves around them and hold the leaves in place with soil or stones, or you can drop the container into a hole dug to size. If plants are damaged despite these precautions, move next year's containers to the south side of a wall or fence where they will be protected from desiccation by wind. A light mulch of pinestraw (that's a southern term; they are called pine needles elsewhere) can help survival, or a mulch of oat or wheat straw. The problem with such straw mulches is that they tend to blow around unless held down by weights or netting.

The degree of winter protection needed by plants depends somewhat on the species being grown. I am continually impressed by the growers of rock garden and alpine plants who leave their precious collections outdoors winter after winter, often in hypertufa containers. (For more on hypertufa, please see Chapter 8.) They depend on persistent snow cover to insulate their plants and to keep them from drying out. I've heard that, in the midst of a prolonged thaw, some hobbyists will go out and shovel snow from residual drifts atop their container plants, not only to protect them from freezing but also to give the soil a good soaking. More plants are lost to drying out during winter than to extreme cold.

■ A cobalt blue urn needs no plant to attract attention. It is set in the
shade of a Japanese maple.

Seven

Herbs and Vegetables in Containers

Herbs

Most herbs are ideally suited to growing in containers. In nature, most grow in well-drained, even dry soils. The mints and a few others are exceptions; they like moderately moist soil. However, you won't go wrong if you use the same moderately fast-draining container mix for all kinds of herbs. Maybe the mints won't grow quite as rapidly in containers as they would in the ground, but on the other hand, you won't have the job of digging their invasive runners out of your garden every few years. In the ground, mints can be spectacularly athletic. If they can't jump over a neighboring plant or go around it, they will grow below or through it. Even in containers you have to keep an eye on them or they will trail down and take root. Give mint its own container. It is as territorial as a German shepherd.

Growing herbs in containers is a win-win situation. You can move containers to near your back door so you can harvest a sprig of this or a soupçon

of that without hoofing it out to the back forty. I know of no other more effective means of increasing your use of herbs in cooking, salads, fruit compotes, and drinks. Also, you can move containers as the season advances and keep ahead of the lengthening shadows. (Most herbs prefer full sun, or at least until midafternoon.) Last but not least, most herbs develop small to medium-sized plants that won't overgrow containers, and the larger-plant herb species are pretty forgiving about being pruned back severely to keep them from flopping all over smaller plants. Lemongrass can replace dracaena or New Zealand flax as a tall specimen for the center of free-standing containers.

A few of the smaller herbs grow fairly well in large hanging baskets, including thyme, sweet marjoram, parsley, salad burnet, chives, and the smaller basils such as 'Spicy Globe.' The mints will thrive in hanging baskets but will need frequent cutting back.

■ Mixed flowers and vegetables in large hanging baskets: Swiss chard 'Bright Lights', hyssop, basil 'Siam Queen', and parsley 'Extra Triple Curled'.

Steer Away from Small Pots

Some gardeners prefer to grow herbs in rather small pots instead of grouped together in large containers. You'll soon discover that small pots dry out quickly and can tip over in a strong breeze and roll around. The root ball will separate from the pot like a spent booster rocket from a space shuttle. You can fill in the blanks from there. Were I to grow herbs in, say, 6-inch pots, I would buy a large terra-cotta basin, set them in it, and fill in around them with sand or small gravel (for weight) to hold the pots in place and to conserve moisture. You can stuff long-fiber florists moss or Spanish moss around the pots for cosmetic purposes. You can feed a collective container of this sort by dissolving fertilizer in a sprinkling can and showering it over plants and filling alike. Very shortly, roots will grow through the drainage holes of your pots and begin extracting water and

■ See how a background of green foliage and understated blossom colors can make a single plant of golden sage stand out.

plant food from the packing around them.

Really Big Strawberry Jars

My favorite container for herbs is a 7- to 10-gallon strawberry jar that will accommodate twelve or more kinds. Strawberry jars are terra-cotta clay jars, narrow at top and bottom, and bulging in the middle. All the staple herbs plus some oddities can sit in a container by the door leading to your kitchen. Visualize that! When I am scheduled for a lecture on landscaping in containers, I check first to see if the auditorium can be darkened to show slides. If not, I prevail upon my sponsor to let me come early to buy plants, containers, and supplies so I can give a demonstration. I am sure that hotels hate to see me come in with my potting soils and plants because they can visualize the mess that I will make on their carpets.

I buy small herb plants for strawberry jars so I can lower them to the desired level inside, and pull their tops through the lipped apertures in the jar. But I'm getting ahead of myself. Before I begin layering potting soil or nursery mix into the jar, I dump it into a clean wheelbarrow and mix in one heaping tablespoon of pelleted dolomitic limestone per gallon of mixture. That amounts to a little less than a half cup for a 5-gallon container and less than a cup for a 7-gallon jar. It's a good time to mix in controlled-release fertilizer as well (unless it is already included in the soil mix).

Follow the directions given on the package. Ignore all the well-meaning admonitions about herbs not needing fertilizer. Nonsense! That advice doesn't make sense when growing them in the ground, much less for in containers. Feed herbs at the rate recommended for herbaceous (soft-bodied) ornamentals, and they will stay in good condition while giving you repeated harvests of vegetative growth. If you liquid-feed, wait for two weeks after planting to let your plants get over transplanting shock.

Basins Give You Lots of Real Estate

My second-choice favorite containers for herbs are broad, rather shallow basins of 5–10 gallon capacity. You get a lot of real estate when you fill a pot that wide . . . lots of room for setting out a variety of plants. You might think that basins dry out faster than tall pots. Not necessarily. Tall pots have a deeper column of water pressing down on a smaller area, thus they drain faster. Yet, the greater surface area of basins will allow faster evaporation unless you mulch around plants with gravel. Your containers are exposed to two different physical phenomena, drainage and evaporation.

When you plant a basin, set in the center the plants that will bush out and

A garden of herbs in a beautiful pot: basil 'African Blue' surrounded by spearmint, golden thyme, and nasturtium, an edible flower.

grow tall as well—common sweet basil, for example. Set the trailers such as thyme and mint out near the rim, but not touching it, or they could dry out too fast. If you can find an even larger basin, you can go for even larger plants— like *Angelica gigas,* the purple one—for the center, or bronze fennel. Whichever size you plant, leave room for a few herbs that have little or no culinary value but have lovely foliage, such as *Artemisia stellarana* 'Silver Brocade' or silver-white curry plant for its appetizing aroma.

Vegetables

You have to keep in mind that some vegetables require so much space to produce a meal at a given harvest that they are not practical for containers. Green beans or peas are good examples. Some vegetables such as sweet corn give you one harvest after 65 days or more of waiting, then have to be pulled out. On the other hand, there are obvious candidates for containers that I call "efficient vegetables." They make efficient use of the area they expand to cover at maturity.

Among the efficient vegetables, it's a toss-up between green peppers and onions from sets as to which can give you the greatest value in fresh produce from a given area in the shortest time span. Tomatoes come close behind them, followed by eggplants. Surprisingly, summer squash comes next. Even though it has big, vigorous leaves, one plant can yield several meals over an extended period of time. At one time, potatoes were so cheap that they were difficult to jus-

tify for gardens in the ground, but have become so dear that they are worth the effort of planting them deep in a wire container and filling in around them with a mixture of decomposed leaves and potting soil as they gain in height. (Don't mix in garden compost; it could transmit potato diseases from previous crops.)

Advanced vegetable gardeners who are good at interplanting and succession-cropping (planting succeeding crops as soon as earlier ones have been harvested) can probably realize the maximum value per unit of space in containers. They do it by starting off with very hardy spinach and onion sets early in the year; interplanting it with leaf lettuce; interplanting the lettuce with green peppers; and sowing turnip, kale, or collard seeds among the peppers for fall harvest. All the greens are fast growing and can be either pulled or clipped for adding to salads or cooking.

Not "Chust for Pretty"

I saw that phrase years ago on a sign in a Pennsylvania Dutch flower garden, and it came to mind as I was scouting through the vegetables in seed catalogs. Some veggies are almost too beautiful to eat. Rainbow colors of Swiss Chard 'Bright Lights'; elegantly tailored, petite

A horse- or mule-drawn one-row seed planter is bedecked with a bi-colored white and green coleus and a dwarf variety of scarlet sage (*Salvia splendens*).

plants of white-stemmed pak-choi; purple-lavender bell pepper 'Islander'; and golden beets are just a few of what noted garden writer Ros Creasy would call Ornamental Edibles. They make sense for balcony, terrace, and patio gardens, where mud-fence-plain vegetables would be more notable for their lack of charm than for their productivity. But were I planting vegetables in half-barrels of manufactured soil as a landscape feature in a yard, I probably would go for efficiency first and charm second. Ever the pragmatist!

The Garbage-Can Method of Growing Tomatoes

I started with a 30-gallon plastic garbage can, drilled drainage holes, filled the can with a soilless mixture, added dolomitic limestone and controlled-release fertilizer, set out one plant of 'Floramerica' tomato, and seventy days later began harvesting the first of what was to total sixty pounds of ripe tomatoes. I set the planted container on bricks for good drainage, surrounded it with a cylinder of reinforcing wire eight feet high, and drove two steel fence posts into the ground to keep the whole contraption from blowing over in a high wind. The tomato vines grew up inside the container, over the top, and goose-necked down another 4 feet!

Since then, a friend and good grower in Augusta, Georgia, continues to chide me because he grew 100 pounds of tomatoes in a 30-gallon container. He mixed two cups of pelleted, dolomitic limestone in a pine-bark-based nursery mix fortified with compost (pasteurized at 140° F), set out two plants of 'Better Boy' hybrid, provided a high cage to keep the vines off the ground, and fed them with Kricket Krap, the edgy trade name for cricket frass produced in Augusta, Georgia. Any way you hack it, 100 pounds of vine-ripened tomatoes is one whale of a crop from such a small area. Awesome! If you want lots of big slicing tomatoes from one or two plants in a container, you have to think big and strong. No wimpy little 5- or 10-gallon containers like you use for peppers, and

no flimsy supports. The breeds of tomatoes labeled "indeterminate" just keep on growing and producing, right up to the first killing frost, and the hybrids called "semi-determinate" in growth habit grow nearly as large. Counting the weight of two vines and fruit, you could have 200 pounds of top growth. Just try standing a plant and container of that size and weight upright after it has blown over. No way! So drive the fence posts in at least a foot deep and fasten the wire cage to them with strong wire.

Turn Your Neighbors Green with Envy

If you live in a neighborhood where each year brings a race to see who harvests the first or the largest tomato, growing them in containers will bring them in earlier than is possible from planting in the ground. You can wrap a double thickness of clear plastic around the cylinder of wire encircling your garbage can and fold in the top to leave only a small chimney for ventilation. Close the opening on cold nights, and lay a blanket over the plastic if frost threatens. With such protection for your tomato plants, you can plant them two or three weeks earlier than it is safe to set plants out in the garden. But growing the largest tomato is a different matter. You have to start with one of the late-maturing varieties that bear relatively few fruit but of astonishingly large size. Even these can be brought to harvest stage earlier with a miniature greenhouse of the type described. Just be sure to remove the plastic covering when the temperature climbs to 70° F, or you will toast your tomatoes, plants and all. Be aware that some of the giant tomato varieties produce terminally ugly fruits: creased, with a deeply indented stem, green shoulders, and sometimes striped or purplish fruit.

Nutritional Value and Taste

I have never detected any difference in the taste of vegetables grown in containers of manufactured soils such as potting soils or container mixes compared to those grown in the ground. No studies have been run on the comparative nutritional values, but I'd venture to guess that they are virtually the same.

Adding Compost and Reusing Soil

You will be tempted, I am sure, to add some good-old homemade compost to the soilless mixes you use for growing tomatoes, peppers, and eggplant in containers, or to reuse the large volume of soil required to grow tomatoes. I would advise you not to do either. Compost, unless it is pasteurized, can carry root-rot organisms and bacterial diseases of

plants. And spent soil, left over from a season of growing, is out of balance nutritionally and out of shape physically. You are better off dumping it on flower beds as a soil conditioner.

■ Two young plants of 'Better Boy' tomatoes just beginning to ripen fruit in the author's garden. They are growing in Fafard Container Mix in a 30-gallon garbage can, and the vines are supported on a cyclone wire fence surrounding a dog run. By the end of the season, these vines should produce at least 50 lbs. of ripe tomatoes.

Eight

Making, Curing, and Planting Lightweight Concrete Hypertufa Containers

Advantages of Lightweight Concrete Hypertufa Containers

Hypertufa (pronounced HY-per-TOO-fah) is a coined word meaning "lighter than tufa," which is a soft, lightweight mineral deposit that can be carved into troughs or sinks and which hardens to look like stone. Hypertufa containers, weighing considerably less than concrete, are relatively portable and can be left outdoors during the winter. Unlike concrete, they quickly take on the patina of age and will blend smoothly into the landscape. Hypertufa containers are usually one of a kind and have a rustic, handmade appearance. If you follow these instructions, your hypertufa containers will be strong and durable. Only in hardiness zone 5 and north will you see a gradual erosion of the surface of your containers caused by the exfoliation (flaking off) that comes with freezing and thawing.

Recommended Sizes and Shapes

Small containers tend to dry out too fast, and overly large containers are too heavy to move with ease. The best compromise is a container with a capacity of 5–20 gallons. Containers of up to 5 gallons capacity are usually made by inverting a pot, tub, or basin and coating it 1½ inches deep with special hypertufa mortar. Spray the inverted form with hair spray and it should slip out of the drying mortar with ease. Larger sizes are usually made in the shape of a trough—rectangular, with the depth being the smallest dimension. A trough with exterior dimensions of 12 inches deep by 18 inches front to back by 24 inches side to side can hold a little less than 2 cubic feet of soil, or about 12 gallons.

■ Hypertufa basin of Japanese forest grass (*Hakonechloa macra* 'Aurea').

Making a Form or Mold for a 12-Gallon Trough

Buy a 4-by-8 sheet of Styrofoam, 2 inches thick, a yardstick to use as a straightedge and razor-blade box opener. Buy a roll of duct tape and a dozen galvanized nails, 4 inches in length. Using a felt-tip pen and a yardstick as a straightedge, lay out the following pieces to minimize waste:

One bottom piece, 22-by-28 inches
Two side pieces, each 12-by-28 inches
Two end pieces, each 12-by-18 inches

Then, follow these steps:

1. Push nails straight through the Styrofoam to mark the corners on the reverse side, and mark the outline.
2. Cut along the lines on both sides. Break off the pieces by bending them over the edge of a table or bench.
3. Assemble the pieces:

■ Footed square hypertufa containers planted with impatiens are sited to flank these steps leading to a shaded area.

a. Set the side pieces on edge and lay the bottom piece atop them.

b. Match up the edges and push nails through the bottom to pin the bottom and sides together.

c. Invert the assemblage and slip the end pieces between sides. Pin them in place.

d. All the edges should be flush. If a piece doesn't fit tightly, pull the nails and trim off projections, then reassemble.

e. Put duct tape on the joints for strength. Don't let the duct tape overlap into the interior of the form.

Recipe for the Mortar

Put on goggles, apron, and gloves. Portland cement is harsh on the skin, eyes, and mucous membranes. Use a coffee can to measure:

2 level cans Portland cement

4 cans Perlite

4 cans brown sphagnum peat moss (pressed down)

2 handfuls of FiberMesh and, if desired, Acryl 60 and pigment according to directions

Only enough water to make a very stiff mortar

Materials for the Hypertufa Mortar

Buy the following materials:

Bag of Portland cement (no sand or gravel); usual weight per bag, 90 pounds

About a cubic foot of FiberMesh, which is short pieces of strong, synthetic fiber for strengthening concrete. Buy it at an outlet for masons' supplies: stone, cement, and such. FiberMesh takes the place of the chicken wire formerly used to add strength.

Large bag of horticultural-grade Perlite (heat-expanded silica) or Vermiculite (heat-expanded mica)

Bale or 3–4 cubic-foot-bag of sphagnum peat moss. Sift out sticks and debris.

Optional Acryl 60 or other acrylic hardener to make the cement more durable and less prone to breakage

A propane torch

Mixing the Mortar

1. Use a water-tight wheelbarrow or a wooden mixing trough.

2. Mix the dry materials, except for the FiberMesh and Acryl 60.

3. Add water in small increments, to make a mortar with the consistency

of drained cottage cheese. Use a garden hoe to blend the ingredients.

4. Scatter the FiberMesh over the wet mortar. Mix it in, along with Acryl 60 and pigment, if desired.

5. Blend the ingredients thoroughly. If the mortar is too soupy, add small amounts of dry ingredients and mix them in.

Applying the Mortar to the Inside of the Form

I prefer to use a narrow, rectangular trowel like the ones used by masons. A garden trowel will suffice.

1. Build up a layer 2 inches thick over the bottom surface. Insert 3 or 4 short pieces of dowel, oiled and wiped dry, to be knocked out later to make drainage holes.

2. Build a layer 1¾ inches thick up the sides, working your way around the perimeter. Round out the inside corners with more mortar to make them stronger.

3. Use a 10-by-12 plywood square as a backstop and a short length of 2-by-4 to firm down the mortar. The 1¾-inch dimension of the 2-by-4 will keep the thickness of the mortar uniform.

4. Make more mortar as needed.

5. When you reach the top of the form, slice off the top, using the edge of the trowel like a saw, then smooth it with the flat of the trowel. On future creations you may wish to scallop or otherwise embellish the edges.

Curing the Trough

Adapt these directions when curing hypertufa pots or tubs.

1. Cover the completed trough with a plastic sheet to retard drying.

2. After 24 hours, strip off the duct tape and pull the pins. Save the forms for later use.

3. Texture the outer surface of the trough, if desired, by scoring it with a scratcher or other iron tool.

4. Slide the trough onto a large square of plywood so two people can carry it. Take it to a shaded area near a water faucet.

5. Fill the form with water and let it sit for two weeks. Keep it covered with plastic to slow the drying process. The longer and slower the drying, the harder the mortar will become.

6. If the trough won't hold water, sprinkle it daily and keep it covered.

7. After two weeks, remove the plastic sheet and let the trough cure in the shade for at least a month before

■ This array of hypertufa pots, urns, basins, tubs, and troughs was made by English Garden Troughs for Cole & Company's use in landscapes. The small inverted dome is a toad house. The long shallow container was made using a bread trough as a mold.

planting. Some gardeners prefer to leave their hypertufa troughs out in the rain and snow all winter before planting them.

8. Knock out the dowels to make drainage holes. Singe off the fibers with a propane torch.

9. Stand back and admire your work of art!

Planting a Hypertufa Trough

Troughs were first used to grow collections of alpine or rock garden plants in areas with cool summers and, during the winter, abundant snow cover. In warmer climes, herbaceous perennial or bulbous species that can stand up to summer heat and humidity are required, and they should be able to withstand short exposures to dry soil. However, this is a relatively new frontier in horticulture, and little research has been done on perennial plants for troughs in hot, humid climates.

The chosen cultivars should be rather small at maturity and slow growing. They can be either woody or herbaceous or both. Plants with colorful foliage or interesting growth habits are especially valuable. For extra protection where winters are short on snow cover, either dig a hole the depth of the container and sink it in to the rim, or bank up garden soil around it. A mulch of evergreen boughs will help your plants survive.★

Of course, you can plant your larger troughs, sinks, or pots with small, well-mannered annuals, and they will look great against the rustic finish of hypertufa. But after a while you may wish to take on the challenge of finding and

planting small-frame perennials, hardy succulents, and bulbous plants for long-term landscape effect.★★

1. Fill the trough to within 2 inches of the rim with a moderately fast-draining potting soil formulated for outdoor containers. Don't add garden soil or fine sand to the potting soil as it could interfere with drainage.

2. Set plants in place and mulch around them with 1 inch of gravel. If you wish, you can imbed several thin pieces of laminar stone (such as flagstone), set on edge and sunk in to various depths. Fill in between them with more potting soil.

3. Water thoroughly. A water wand that will deliver a fine spray works better than a hose nozzle that can blast small plants out of the soil.

4. In areas with hot summers, set the container where it will receive afternoon shade.

5. If your plants are stunted or yellow, it may be because of inadequate curing, resulting in a high level of alkalinity. Leave the container outdoors through the winter, and the alkalinity will drop to safe levels. Try feeding your plants with a solution of liquid fertilizer containing micronutrients before assuming that alkalinity is the cause of the problem.

★Panyoti Keliades, curator of Rock Gardens at the Denver Botanic Gardens, has overwintered troughs for many years in this fashion. He and his wife, Gwen, are longtime members of the Rock Garden Society and grow many plants in troughs. I was the presenter when Panyoti was featured in one of the Great Gardeners programs aired over HGTV.

★★One of the best reference books on small, winter-hardy herbaceous and woody plants for planting in hypertufa troughs and sinks is *Creating and Planting Garden Troughs,* by Joyce Fingerut and Rex Murfitt, published by B. B. Mackey Books, P.O. Box 475, Wayne, PA 19087.

■ The small hypertufa pot in the foreground has a flared bottom to give it a dog-dish shape and is mulched with native Utah pebbles. The featured plant is in scale with this size of pot.

Care and Feeding of Plants in Hypertufa Containers

Feed and water plants in hypertufa containers, just as you would those growing in clay or plastic pots. You can mix long-lasting controlled-release fertilizer with your potting soil for season-long feeding, or feed your plants every week or two with a solution of water-soluble fertilizer fortified with micronutrients. First, however, read the copy on the back of the package of soil: controlled-release fertilizers may have already been added. You might wish to elevate your containers on bricks or "feet" cast from hypertufa mortar. When containers are set up off the ground, tree roots can't invade them from below.

Nine

Condensed Encyclopedia of Modern Plants Adapted to Container Growing

This is a short list of my favorites among the many flowers that will grow well in containers. Without a doubt many more kinds deserve mention, but I haven't seen or grown them and would feel uncomfortable proclaiming their virtues. In the following descriptions, foliage colors will be mentioned only if the plant is grown principally for its foliage, or if the foliage is particularly attractive or novel. Also note that I used the word "moderately" in describing plants resistant to heat and humidity. Some regions in the U.S. have either prolonged, intense heat night and day or oppressive humidity, both of which narrow the choice of plants that will thrive in containers. Also, some kinds don't fit neatly into one of the three categories I use to describe plant habits: low, mounding, or tall. A certain amount of overlap is unavoidable. Finally, before you become confused by finding some heat-tolerant kinds listed under cool-summer flowers or vice versa, blame it on my desire to be helpful. Many kinds are so adaptable to a wide range of climates that they can't fit perfectly into either category.

You will see Proven Winners mentioned in several descriptions. This is a trade organization that evaluates vegetatively propagated cultivars in various sites across the country and promotes their sale. Promising cultivars are dubbed Proven Winners. All-America Selections awards for certain varieties are mentioned. AAS has been active in evaluating seed-grown flowers, vegetables, and herbs since 1932. A third trade organization, FloraStar, evaluates new introductions for their adaptability to pot plant culture, but many of their winners perform superbly when grown in the ground. Last but not least, the Perennial Plant Association annually announces its Perennial Plant of the Year award.

Often as not, their awards go to deserving plants that have been marketed for a number of years.

Plant variety patents are used mainly for vegetatively propagated plants and are signified by the letters "PP" followed by a patent number. "PPAF" stands for Plant Patent Applied For.

To help you make shopping lists of cultivars for planting in containers, I have classified them rather loosely by plant habit and tolerance for heat and humidity. As you choose from this list, be sure to group shade-tolerant or sun-tolerant flowers with others of their kind.

Low-Growing, Trailing Plants, Moderately Resistant to Heat and Humidity

Artemisia or wormwood (*Artemisia* sp.) All the artemisias like the well-drained, seldom-soggy soil in containers. Most of the species available at retail are hardy perennials grown more for their silvery-green, deeply cut foliage than for their flowers. Some, such as 'Silver King', spread rapidly by underground runners and are too tall and rambunctious for containers. Others such as 'Silver Mound' grow rather slowly to form small plants that coexist peaceably with other species in containers. One of my favorites is *A. stellarana* 'Silver Brocade', which hugs the ground and will extend gracefully over the rims of containers. Grow in full sun.

'Blue Daze' (*Evolvulus pilosus*) It is a tossup whether this plant belongs here or among the mounding types. I put it among the trailing plants because by midseason it forms short runners that tumble over the rims of containers or hanging baskets. 'Blue Daze' makes attractive gray-green, drought-resistant plants that are spangled with small, deep blue flowers resembling miniature morning glories. The modern variety 'Hawaiian Blue Eyes' has slightly larger

■ **Hanging basket of strawberry firetails (*Acalypha pendula*).**

flowers. Blossoms are open only when the sun is shining. With protection, plants will live over in zone 8 and south. Grow in full sun or light shade.

Firetails (*Acalypha pendula*) You will often see this one growing in hanging baskets, with its furry, rose-red "tails" hanging from the tips of branches. The tails aren't long, and the centers of the plants are all green, so it would be a waste to plant firetails where it could not be seen from below. Sometimes confused with chenille plant (*A. hispida*), but true chenille plant is shrubby and much larger, with long ribbons of flowers like chenille. Resistant to heat and humidity; grow as an annual in full sun or light shade.

Dahlberg daisy (*Thymophylla tenuiloba,* formerly *Dyssodia tenuiloba*) I could hardly believe my eyes when I saw this species blooming in intense heat in Arizona. The 8-inch-high plants look delicate, with trailing, ferny branches and tiny yellow daisy blossoms in great numbers. Since then I have been seeing Dahlberg daisy over much of the country, growing as a filler flower in containers. It will trail slightly, just enough to soften the hard edges of containers. Hot weather combined with prolonged high humidity can burn it out in late summer. In cool climates Dahlberg daisies can be combined with blue lobelias for an eye-catching effect. Annual.

False licorice (*Helichrysum petiolatum*) This is an extremely popular plant that weaves in between mounding plants and extends its descending branches from containers and hanging baskets.

■ Cast-stone basket holds individual pots of lantana, false licorice, nierembergia 'Mt. Blanc', petunias, and dracaena for a temporary show.

Most often you will see the silvery-gray, round-leafed cultivar, but lime-green, variegated, and little-leafed cultivars are becoming available. These former two plants don't trail, but grow straight out before most appealingly bending down and arching back up. The little-leafed cultivar 'Petite' grows so slowly that it is used mostly as a filler. By the season's end it assumes the form of a small shrub. Full sun or light shade. Perennial in hardiness zone 9 and south, grow as an annual elsewhere.

Fan flower (*Scaevola aemula*) This relative newcomer surprised everyone with its heat resistance, but it needs plenty of water and good drainage to stay in condition. Spreads slowly to billow over the sides of containers and hanging baskets. Fleshy stems are brittle;

■ The bluish purple blooms of *Scaevola* look like the blades of a fan.

■ Clay basin with chameleon plant (*Houttynia* sp.), portulaca not yet in bloom, and hen and chicks.

grow it away from strong winds. Comes in blue, pink, or white cultivars and blooms almost all summer. Full sun or light shade. Grow as an annual.

Harlequin vine (*Houttuynia cordata*) I'd rather see this one in containers than planted in the ground because it has potential for becoming invasive. It hugs the ground while spreading, and will drape down nicely. Its flowers are insignificant, but no matter, because the brightly variegated foliage doesn't need any help. The heart-shaped leaves are green with red, maroon, and yellow markings. Dump out the plants at season's end and heel them in; with any luck they will survive the winter. Grow in light to moderate shade.

Lantana (*L. montevidensis*) The little-leafed, trailing lantana cultivars bred from *L. montevidensis*, or the compact-plant 'Cowboy' cultivars are what you want for hanging baskets. They will grow about 18 inches tall while spreading to twice as wide. Large baskets of 5 gallons or greater capacity are needed to display

The designer of this planting made a good choice of lantana color to go with this "instant antique" wheelbarrow.

lantana properly. Trailing lantana comes in blue and white combinations and in pure white. Some new hybrids include colors from the shrubby, yellow–orange *L. camara*. Somewhere, breeders found a lovely pink color to breed into the vigorous, bushy 'Athens Rose'. Lantana is arguably the most heat- and humidity-resistant flower available, and draws myriad butterflies and hummingbirds as well. Caution: if the plant you are considering buying has large leaves, it may grow too big for containers. Wear gloves when handling lantana; it can cause temporary itching. Grow in full sun. Perennial in zone 8 and south. The shrubby 'Miss Huff' will live over in zone 7.

Lysimachia (*L. congestiflora* and *L. procumbens*) "Variegated" seems inadequate to describe *L. congestiflora* 'Outback Sunset'. Its strong cream and gold edging is highly visible in a lightly shaded area, as are its ball-like clusters of yellow flowers. Low-growing, spreading, and heat-resistant, this cultivar is rapidly gaining in popularity. *L. procumbens*

■ Hanging baskets of purple 'Million Bells', pink star cluster flower, golden coreopsis, and false licorice.

shade. I have found 'Eco Dark Satin' to be more tolerant of full sun. Grow as annuals.

Million Bells (*Calibrachoa* hybrids) At first, I called this recent introduction a near-petunia, because its blossoms look like miniature petunias. But after growing it through a season, I must say it is anything but. The leaves of Million Bells are much smaller and slimmer than those of petunias and don't have the distinctive aroma. The slim plants start out growing vertically, but soon branch so much that their weight causes them to arch and descend to a foot or more in length. Blooms come without letup, and as they fade, they drop off cleanly, leaving small, green, star-shaped bracts rather than spent flowers in various stages of deterioration. New branches continually form near the center of the plants so they never have a bare "bald spot." The 1-inch, bell-shaped flowers come in six soft colors: two shades of pink, plus violet-blue, white, yellow, and a yellow bicolor called 'Terra Cotta'. Another series of *Calibrachoa* hybrids have been given the name 'Lyricashowers'. They, too, come in several colors and have slightly larger flowers than the 'Million Bells' series. Both series are more frost-tolerant than petunias. Grow in full sun; treat as an annual.

'Golden Globes' has green foliage and yellow clusters of blossoms much like those of 'Outback Sunset', and trails nicely in hanging baskets. Both flourish in hot weather if given light to moderate shade. If 'Outback Sunset' tends to parch around leaf margins, move it to deeper

Osteospermum or freeway daisy

■ Dandenong daisy or *Dimorphotheca* 'Rose' (PPAF) is a spreading plant that holds its many-petalled blossoms well above the foliage.

(*Osteospermum* cultivars) I've seen the new osteospermums in a number of trials and consider them best suited to hot, dry climates. When they receive a lot of rain or irrigation, they grow lanky and floppy. One way to grow them dry in rainy climates would be to plant them in hanging baskets beneath eaves. The blossoms are truly beautiful, either white with a purple blush on the lower surfaces, or solid purple or crimson, with many-petalled daisy flowers. Dandenong daisies grow like the osteospermums but

have flowers in warm colors. The lax branches will tumble over the rims of hanging baskets. Grow in full sun or afternoon shade. Treat as an annual.

Parrot's Beak (*Lotus berthelotii*) A most unusual trailer with lacy, silvery foliage and bright red blossoms shaped like the beak of a parrot, except fancier. Hot weather stops the formation of flowers but then the attractive foliage visually takes over. It is often seen planted alone in baskets or trailing over the edge of large containers. I saw one at the Missouri

New Guinea impatiens, parrot's beak (*Lotus berthelotii*), dracaena, and streptocarpella 'Concord Blue'.

Botanical Garden that had trailed down more than 3 feet by the season's end. Grow in full sun. Frost-tender.

Petunias (*Petunia* hybrids) "You've come a long way, baby!" I can remember when, ages ago, 'Fire Chief' was introduced, the first true red petunia. It won an All-America Selections award. Now, a whole new class of 'Wave' petunias offers a low-growing, mat-forming plant habit. 'Purple Wave', a stunning, deep reddish-purple, keeps on blooming through summer heat. 'Pink Wave' came next, but my favorite is 'Misty Lilac Wave' in a soft, almost faded, lavender pink. Don't confuse these with the 'Tidal Wave' color series, which has taller, larger plants. Now, the 'Surfinia' class of trailing petunias is giving the 'Wave' cultivars a run for the money. 'Surfinias' come in many colors, including two with contrasting deep purple throats and veining. The 'Surfinias' are vegetatively propagated by Proven Winners and are either patented or under PPAF. I am told that the ancestor of the 'Surfinias' was discovered in a

Brazilian vineyard. All petunias need full sun and are relatively drought-resistant. Annual except in zone 9 and south.

Purple heart (*Tradescantia pallida,* formerly *Setcreasea pallida*) A common name for this deep purple plant is Wandering Jew but that name is in general use for zebrina (*Tradescantia zebrina*). I like its other common name, purple heart, much better. The fleshy plants have long, purple, trough-shaped leaves on spreading runners that will trail down from hanging baskets. The surface of the foliage is waxy and doesn't catch and hold rain or irrigation water. The light purple blossoms are small and not especially showy. Because of its odd leaf shape and angular growth, purple heart looks best when planted by itself in 5-gallon containers. It is a very tough, drought-resistant plant that can recover from neglect. Full sun or light shade. Perennial in hardiness zone 8 and south.

Spanish daisy (*Erigeron karvinskianus*) Don't let the jawbreaker name put you off. This is one of the nicest spreading, daisy-flowered plants you can buy, and it blooms all summer long. It is a short-lived perennial, usually grown as an annual, with plants that average 1 foot in height and 2 feet across. The small, semidouble blossoms are borne in great numbers. They start off white and age to

An elegant old concrete container is gathering a patina of algae and moss. Planted with trailing plectranthus, pentas, and purple heart (*Tradescantia pallida*).

pink and lavender, giving the plant a multicolored appearance. 'Profusion' is a choice variety. Full sun or light shade.

Swedish ivy or plectranthus (*Plectranthus australis*) This and other species of plectranthus are nearly as popular as vinca vine for hanging baskets and for trailing over the edges of free-standing containers. Cultivars offer several variations in leaf sizes, shapes, and in green and white, or green and cream color variegations, and dark purple. Leaves and stems are fleshy and a bit brittle; therefore, protect plantings from strong winds. If you want trailing plants, buy

■ Several potted plants sit in this antique wheelbarrow. The daisylike flower is *Erigeron karvinskianus*.

the plectranthus with runners. You'll see runners on certain of the cultivars even when plants are young. Some cultivars such as the silvery-gray one (mysteriously called 'Brazilian coleus') form mounds of foliage with no runners. Grow in moderate shade where summers are quite hot. Usually grown as an annual.

Sweet potatoes (*Ipomoea batatas*) Who would have dreamed that sweet

potatoes could become a major plant for hanging baskets and for large containers? It's the new foliage colors that did it. Plant breeders selected for lime-green ('Marguerita'), chocolate ('Blackie'), and tricolor foliage. My personal favorite is the tricolor (light green, cream, pink and, late in the season, purple) because it doesn't grow as fast as the other two. The recently introduced 'Black Heart' looks great, too. The sweet potatoes quickly produce long, trailing vines that can be clipped if they become unmanageable. Grow ornamental sweet potatoes in 20-inch hanging baskets or in containers of 10-gallon size and up. You might not be able to buy them in a few southern counties where a sweet potato quarantine is in effect because of sweet potato weevil. Full sun. Frost-tender.

Verbena (*Verbena* hybrids) Collectively, the modern verbenas make up one of the most important classes of flowers for containers. They are more heat-resistant than annual verbenas and are less troubled by leaf miners and mildew. (Leaf miners are insects whose grubs tunnel through the inner cells of leaves, leaving brown tracks.) Accidental hybrids, reportedly between *V. canadensis* and *V. rigida,* grew for years along southeastern roadsides until noticed by horticulturists and introduced. The deep purple 'Homestead' was the first, followed by several more colors, including my favorite, the lavender 'Abbeville'. All are vigorous and wide-spreading, and bloom in "flushes" throughout the summer, resting up between performances. 'Homestead' begins blooming very early. I shouldn't have the temerity to guess at plant parentage, but it appears that breeders may have then introduced *V.*

■ **The dependable trailing variegated plectranthus in the large-leafed, green and white form.**

tenuisecta, a lacy-leafed species, into crosses to come up with several colors under the 'Tapien' class. These plants are smaller than the early introductions and have ferny leaves along with some unusual colors, such as powder blue. Proven Winners introduced the broadleafed 'Temari' series in several colors. Yet another verbena has possibilities for a mound-forming plant in containers, the Great Plains wildflower, *V. bipinnatifida.*

■ An extraordinary combination of variegated elderberry (*Sambucus nigra* 'Madonna'), verbena 'Freefalls Purple', sweet potato 'Blackie' and 'Marguerita', and angel flower (*Angelonia angustifolia* 'Hilo Princess').

It has lavender-pink blossoms and a bushy plant habit. The dependable fern-leaf species *V. tenuisecta* is often used in containers for its finely cut, wispy foliage and purple blossoms. Full sun. Most of these verbena cultivars are perennial in hardiness zone 7 and south.

Vinca vine or vine myrtle (*V. major* and *V. minor*) A variegated version of the fast-growing, large-leafed *V. major* is perhaps the most popular trailing plant for containers. Its glossy foliage hangs down like leafy strings that can reach 3 to 4 feet in length where summers are long and bears blue flowers in the spring. *V. minor* has smaller, slower-growing plants with narrow leaves. Vinca comes in purple, blue, white, and pink-flowered cultivars, and in a variegated form. A hard-to-find cultivar has dark red stems. Light to moderate shade. Hardy through zone 6.

■ Hanging baskets of streptocarpella, variegated vinca vine (*V. major* 'Variegata'), ivy, and strawberry firetails (*Acalypha pendula*).

■ Verbena 'Freefalls Lavender', periwinkle 'Cascade Pink', and a mixed-colors impatiens.

■ Tuberous-rooted begonias and lobelias grow beautifully in the mild New Zealand climate, with its cool nights and long growing seasons.

Low-Growing, Trailing Plants That Prefer Cool Summers

Anagallis or **pimpernel** (*A. monelli*) I like this one for its intense deep violet–blue blossoms with yellow stamens. The blossoms aren't large, but literally cover the plant from late spring through fall frost where summers are cool. The plants start out as mounds but spread to hang over the rims of hanging baskets or troughs. Try combining it with yellow flowers to show off the rich, deep blue. Full sun or light shade. Annual.

Begonia, tuberous-rooted (pendulous *Begonia* hybrids) The pendulous hybrids don't actually trail, but hang over the edge of hanging baskets to show off their large, vivid, pendent blossoms. You will see mostly single-flowered or semi-double kinds in stores, already in bloom, ready to take home and hang up. Ask your dealer to stock the double-flowered 'Show Angels'. It comes in several soft colors, with each petal penciled around the margins with dark red. Grow in moderate shade and with protection from wind, as the plants are brittle. You will see these begonias for sale in southern stores, but if you buy them, be advised that they can't tolerate much heat. Grow as an annual.

Lady's mantle (*Alchemilla mollis*) Sometimes sold as an herb, lady's mantle makes a lovely, shade-tolerant, hardy perennial foliage plant for concrete or hypertufa containers that are to remain in the garden over winter. It grows rather slowly but within a season will begin to trail over the rims of troughs or sinks. Poets wax ecstatic over the way dew or rain rolls into prismatic droplets that collect in the cupped leaves and reflect light. The small sprays of yellow flowers are a bonus. I've seen it grown as far south as zone 8 but it grows larger and more vigorously further north. Full sun to moderate shade in the North; moderate shade in the South.

Lobelia, trailing (*Lobelia erinus*) The trailing lobelias are among the best cool-summer flowers. They keep on blooming as they billow over the sides of hanging baskets and hang down 6 to 12 inches. The dark-flowered kinds tend to have dark foliage. 'Sapphire', deep blue with a white eye, may be the best known. You can occasionally find plants of the deep carmine 'Ruby Cascade' or 'Red Cas-

■ **The home gardeners of Ashburton, New Zealand, rival those of Christchurch and Auckland in their yearly competition for the best gardens. This home utilized space on its carport walls to display tuberous begonias, lobelia, petunias, and fuchsia.**

cade', and the cobalt blue *L. tenuior* 'Blue Wings'. Lobelia flowers look like tiny snapdragons and can nearly hide the foliage. Full sun to light shade. Annual.

Laurentia (*Solenopsis* sp., *Laurentia axillaris*) With the introduction of the fragrant 'Blue Stars' a few years ago, laurentia began attracting attention all over the world. Then along came the white 'Shooting Stars'. I saw them first at the Park Seed performance trials near my home, then a few weeks later at the display beds at the Minnesota Landscape

This die-cast concrete urn is planted with conventional garden flowers: nicotiana, lobelia, and blue laurentia.

Arboretum. Both plantings were spectacular, but the northern planting stayed in condition until frost. The plants grow 6 to 12 inches high and twice as wide, forming compact masses of tiny leaves, covered with distinctive one-sided blossoms with five narrow, sharply pointed petals. Plant laurentia near the rims of large containers and let it tumble over. Full sun to light shade. Annual.

Nasturtium (*Tropaeolum majus*) I wouldn't settle for common nasturtiums but would send for seeds of a new trailing, double-flowered variety such as the orange 'Hermine Grashoff', or the variegated 'Alaska Mixed Colors', which are

■ Here's a display of choice container plants: a double-flowered nasturtium, yucca, fuchsia, variegated plectranthus, a slender species of scouring rush (*Equisetum*), and various succulents.

more tumblers than trailers. Tumblers billow over the rims of containers while trailers tend to hang straight down. Nasturtiums grow rapidly from seeds and will begin blooming within a few weeks, or you can purchase seedlings in pots. Modern varieties hold their flowers above the foliage instead of hiding them beneath a green canopy. Grow in full sun, and if pruning is required, eat the clippings. Bon appetit!

Mound-Shaped Plants, Moderately Resistant to Heat and Humidity

Angel flower (*Angelonia angustifolia*), sometimes labeled summer snapdragon. I've never before seen a plant catch on so fast. Long grown in the Deep South, it was picked up by buyers for mass marketers and quickly became established all over the eastern U.S. It has slender, upright branches topped with short spikes of snapdragonlike flowers, but overall, the plant form is mounded. The most

■ Footed half-barrel with chartreuse false licorice, *Helichrysum* 'Dargan Hill Monarch', *Bidens* 'Golden Goddess', and trailing vine.

containers, and individual plants will grow to more than 2 feet wide and nearly as tall in one season. It has large, wing-shaped, green-bronze leaves with sawtooth edges, and loads of large, scarlet blossoms. Quite heat-resistant in full sun in the North, but likes light to moderate shade in the South. Grow as an annual. You can overwinter cuttings as house plants.

Bidens (*B. ferulifolia*) 'Peters Golden Carpet'. This cultivar performs well in University of Georgia trials in containers and landscape beds. Other *Bidens* (tickseed) species are regularly grown as roadside wildflowers but have never made it in strength to home gardens. This little gem puts you in mind of the great favorite, *Coreopsis verticillata* 'Moonbeam' but has smaller, less spreading plants, and its leaves are heavier, more lobed than needlelike. Its simple, daisylike, golden blossoms are small but numerous. Use it as a filler flower among more dense plants. A short-lived perennial usually grown as an annual. Full sun to light shade.

available color is purple with white markings. Recently, Ball FloraPlant introduced their vegetatively produced, virus-free AngelMist series, which includes the varieties 'Deep Plum', 'Lavender', 'Pink', 'Purple Stripe', and 'White'. Resistant to heat and humidity. Grow in full sun. Annual.

Begonia x 'Dragon Wing'. I don't know the parentage of this hybrid, but it doesn't matter. It is simply one of the most beautiful, widely adapted, consistent performers that I have seen during the past fifty years. It likes the good drainage provided by soilless mixes in

Coreopsis (*Coreopsis verticillata* and *C. grandiflora*) The pale yellow 'Moonbeam', one of the threadleaf coreopsis, is one of the great hardy perennials of all time. It and its golden sister, 'Zagreb', both grow well in large containers, rewarding you with all-summer

■ Mary Alice Keoh of Milwaulkee took this snapshot of a very old cast iron container, perhaps once used for watering horses, standing in a traffic divider in Hingham, Massachusetts. Planted with the silvery dusty miller, marigolds, *Bidens* sp. 'Golden Goddess', fan flower, blue salvia (center of container), white impatiens, and verbena.

color. If you want smaller plants, try one of the compact varieties of the short-lived perennial *C. grandiflora*, such as 'Sunray'. It grows to only 12 inches high and doesn't spread vigorously like older varieties, but its foliage is a bit heavier than that of the threadleaf types and its flowers are more showy. Full sun.

Dusty miller Selections from three genera: *Artemisia, Senecio,* and *Cineraria,* go by this common name. All have silvery-gray foliage, varying from oblong to deeply cut, even feathery, depending on the cultivar. Only *A. stellarana* 'Silver Brocade' is mat forming and trailing. All prefer excellent drainage and can tolerate intense sun. Container gardeners consider these as staples for calming colors that otherwise might clash. 'Cirrus' and 'Silver Brocade' often live through the winter in hardiness zone 7 and may be hardy in protected gardens further north. Grow in full sun.

Gaillardia or blanket flower (*Gaillardia aristata*) Often, when plant breeders dwarf a vigorous native plant species, the miniature version loses vigor and heat resistance. Not so with Gaillardia 'Goblin'. This little imp is as tough as rawhide and will flourish on soil so poor a rabbit

Plant breeding has trimmed the rangy plants of heliotrope to produce the compact *Heliotropium arborescens* 'Atlantis' (PPAF) for pot culture. Flowers are vanilla-scented.

has to carry his lunch when he crosses it. Technically a short-lived perennial, 'Goblin' blooms early and continuously the first year on plants 12 inches high. On sandy soil, it will drop seeds and come back for years. Its single, daisylike blossoms come in warm bicolors that show well against the gray-green, lobed foliage. Use the standard-sized tall varieties of blanket flower and the related Indian blanket in large containers.

Geranium 'Golden Ear' (*Pelargonium* x 'Golden Ear') This tough little plant is grown mostly for its deep golden leaves, strongly marked with chocolate brown. The margins of leaves appear to have been cut with pinking shears. It grows no more than a foot high and about the same width, and has unremarkable scarlet blossoms. Planted in a 5-gallon Mexican clay container in my garden, it stood up to one of the hottest summers on record. It looks best when featured alone in a pot, as its coloration is so theatrical that it wouldn't blend well with other flowers. Full sun. Grow as an annual. You can carry rooted cuttings through the winter as houseplants.

Heliotrope (*Heliotropium arborescens*) Want fragrance in your containers? The common name of heliotrope, cherry pie plant, accurately describes its scent, though some writers ascribe a vanilla scent to it. The broad, flattened flower heads of 'Mini Marine' are an intense, very dark purple, and they show off well

A half-barrel planted with hostas and a wildflower known as green and gold (*Chrysogonum virginianum*).

against the medium green, corrugated leaves. 'Blue Wonder Hybrid' is a lighter violet blue and has 15-inch high plants, a bit taller than 'Mini Marine'. A white-flowered variety is also available. All grow well in containers. Deadhead the spent flowers. Try combining purple heliotrope with one of the orange dwarf French marigolds for a smashing color contrast. Grow as an annual, in full sun or light shade.

Hosta (*Hosta* cultivars) The leading shade-tolerant hardy perennial, hostas also make good container plants. The dainty edging types combine well with other shade-loving flowers such as lamium and dwarf plumbago (*Ceratostigma plumbaginoides*), and the culti-

vars with medium-sized plants look good when planted by themselves in 5-gallon containers. I doubt if the world is ready for some of the huge specimen hostas in containers; some of them flower at a height of 4 feet and spread wider than I can span with my arms. At the end of the growing season you can dump out containers and heel in hostas for replanting the following season. Light to moderate shade.

Impatiens (*I. wallerana* and *I. hawkeri* hybrids) What can one say about the most popular bedding plants in North America? You already know that they bloom all summer long in light shade (moderate in the South), that they come in a bewildering choice of colors, and

■ Another barrel planter with New Guinea impatiens, fan flower 'Blue Wonder', and chartreuse false licorice.

that they attract butterflies. I can only re-mind you that the standard impatiens can withstand more shade than the New Guinea hybrids, and that despite the hype about their liking full sun, New Guinea impatiens prefer light to moder-ate shade, especially in the South, and misting during hot, dry weather. Impa-tiens won't grow well where the air is hot and dry. The 1-foot high plants grow too large for small containers and are best combined with other shade-tolerant flowers in large containers. Be frugal with plant food and water; both types of impatiens can grow too leggy and de-velop foliage at the expense of flowers if pampered. Frost-tender.

Joseph's coat (*Alternanthera ficoidea*) Not to be confused with the tall, showy amaranthus that goes by the same com-mon name, the many cultivars of this species have low-growing plants that can be pruned severely to make living floral designs. Solid red or pink cultivars are available, but most gardeners prefer the variegated types: green and white, green and orange-red, and yellow and purple. I grow the slender-leafed little green and yellow cultivar 'Frizzy'. It isn't daunted by prolonged heat and high humidity. Despite the durability and ease of growth of the alternantheras through hot, humid weather, retailers seldom carry a good selection of cultivars, perhaps because it is a foliage plant and doesn't have showy flowers. Nevertheless, it is one of the best mounding plants for containers and will trail by late summer. It has small leaves and limber branches. Frost-tender; grow in full sun.

■ **Basin of dwarf celosia, French marigolds, and butter daisy, *Melampodium paludosum*.**

Melampodium or **butter daisy** (*M. paludosum*) One of the most dependable yellow-flowered, heat- and humidity-resistant annuals has been improved by seed breeders. The somewhat similar varieties 'Derby' and the more recent 'Million Gold' have compact plants that begin blooming early and continue through the summer. They mature at a height of about 10 inches and can tolerate occasional neglect. The older, unimproved varieties grow too large for container culture. Full sun to light shade.

Mickey Mouse plant or **bat flower** (*Ochna serrulata*) I doubt if Walt Disney Productions had anything to do with naming this plant, but one close-up look at a flower will impress you with its similarity to a Mouseketeer's cap. Some gardeners feel it looks more like the face

of a bat. More than just a curiosity, this robust plant is a solid performer in hot weather and is not killed by light frosts. Its flowers are less than an inch in diameter, with red "ears" and near-black "cap." In my garden, it has narrow leaves on mounded plants 2 feet high by 2 feet wide, but I would guess it would grow larger further south. Grow in full sun; treat as an annual.

Peppers, ornamental (*Capsicum frutescens*) Grow these flashy little plants for their colorful, edible, usually hot fruit. Depending on the variety, fruit may be round, tapered, thin and curvy, or cigar-shaped. Fruit colors change as they ripen. Some shift from green and yellow to orange or red, while others start off

■ An old horse-drawn seed planter, this one for multiple rows, sports cascading red and white grandiflora petunias at the Antique Mall, Donalds, South Carolina.

green and mature a deep purple. Some varieties like 'Jigsaw' have purple/white variegated foliage. The bright colors of the yellow/red ornamental peppers shout so loudly that one plant is sufficient for a mixed planting in a large container. Snip off branch tips to keep your plants tidy and globe-shaped. Most varieties have pungent fruit, but if children visit your garden, sweet-fruited kinds are available. Grow in full sun. Annual north of zone 10.

Petunias (*Petunia* hybrids) All the wonderful new grown-from-seeds hybrid petunias belong in this class. Al-though breeders continue to bring the new hybrids down in height, most are taller than the 'Wave' and 'Surfinia' types (see page 94) and can be used in either free-standing containers or hanging baskets. Almost every flower color except brown and black is represented in this class. In blossom size the 'Grandifloras' are the largest. The 'Multifloras' have slightly smaller blossoms but are more resistant to botrytis mold. Smallest of all are the Milleflora petunias. The 'Fantasy' series belongs to this class. Its plants and blossoms are so small that you are reminded of the movie *Honey, I Shrunk the*

Basins give you comparatively more planting space than standard pots of the same cubic capacity. This one is planted with 'Green Splash' polka-dot plant, marigolds, fan flower, pentas, and narrow-leafed zinnias. Come nightfall, they will snap back from the slight wilting effect of the afternoon sun.

Petunias! The seven colors of 'Supertunias' are propagated vegetatively, and despite their trailing habit, they don't hug the ground like the 'Wave' series. They are all patented and offered by Proven Winners.

Polka-dot plant (*Hypoestes phyllostachya*) Here is a dandy little shade-tolerant foliage plant. Recently improved by plant breeders, its four colors are brighter than the original offerings. Pink, white, red, or rose flecking is interspersed with green. I often use polka-dot plants in my demonstrations, mixing them with flowering species. The plants color up when tiny and continue to grow in height all summer long. You may

need to cut them back if they overgrow your container. Very resistant to heat and humidity. Give them light to moderate shade. Also adapted to northern gardens, but there the plants rarely grow more than 8 inches tall. Grow as an annual.

Rose moss or **portulaca** (*Portulaca* spp.) It would be hard to find a flower to match portulaca for tolerance of dry soil and heat. Yet, it does grow significantly better with regular watering and light fertilization. The plants start out mound-shaped but where summers are long, they sprawl out to 8 inches high by 2 feet across. Thanks to the perseverance of seed breeders, the 'Sundial' series of a dozen or so colors stays open much

■ Euro-American Propagators plants dozens of combinations, including many proven winners along with old favorites in containers to demonstrate the potential of plants for containers. That's tricolor sage (*Salvia officinalis* 'Tricolor') in the square container in the foreground.

longer than old-fashioned varieties. The petals have a silken sheen and a clarity of color that is special to rose moss. Portulaca has small, fleshy, sausage-shaped leaves on brittle stems. A related flower known as purslane has fleshy leaves, much larger than those of rose moss. Its

'Yubi' series of colors is especially prized for heat resistance. Use either species as a filler flower in containers. Grow on dry soil in full sun; shade affects blooming. Frost-tender annual.

Sage, tricolor (*Salvia officinalis*)
What a performer! This plant started out

as plain gray garden sage but fell in a paint pot along the way. Even its seedlings show three foliage colors: gray-green, cream, and pink. Plant three seedlings in a 3-gallon pot and watch them billow over the edge. Replace one sage with a plant of silver santolina and see how the plain foil brings out the fancy coloration of the sage. But if you are looking for an herbal companion for blue flowers, go for golden sage, which has green and creamy yellow variegated leaves. For a big sage plant that can stand alone in containers, select 'Bergartten'. Grow the sages with excellent drainage. They may need supplemental pelleted limestone in soft-water areas. Full sun. These are short-lived perennials, usually grown as annuals.

Sedum (*Sedum* sp.) Most gardeners know the hardy perennial sedums, especially the late-blooming, 2-feet-high 'Autumn Glory' that is attractive at all stages of growth. Now it has a rival for the affection of sedum lovers: 'Matrona', which wowed all Europe in its trials. 'Matrona' has purple stems, fleshy, greenish-purple leaves, and large clusters of pink flowers. Established plants grow several upright stems about 1 1/2 feet in height. Both cultivars are attractive to butterflies and should be grown in full sun or light shade.

Star cluster flower (*Pentas lanceolata*) The very compact 'New Look' variety of pentas forms globe-shaped plants only 8–10 inches in height, a good size for containers. The little plants are not quite as resistant to weather stresses as the much taller standard pentas, and they are fairly expensive because they require up to five months from seed sowing to bloom. Five colors are available: pink, red, white, lavender, and violet, all of which are irresistible to butterflies and hummingbirds. The standard tall pentas can grow 2–4 feet tall in one season, and I've seen perennial plants in coastal Southern California growing taller than my head! Watch for the new seed-grown F_1 hybrid 'Butterfly' pentas. They reach 12–18 inches in height at maturity and come in several colors. Pentas are grown as annuals in zone 9 and north. Full sun.

Strawflower (*Helichrysum bracteatum*) One of the selections from the same genus as the old-fashioned tall strawflower that was grown for drying and use in arrangements is short, spreading, and light golden in color. Proven Winners introduced it as 'Golden Beauty'. It blooms all summer long, but benefits from occasional shearing and feeding. Grows to a height of about 1 foot and spreads twice as wide. Very

■ Strawflower (*Helichrysum bracteatum* 'Golden Beauty') with one of the Temari verbenas, 'Bright Red', which has been outstanding in trials across the country. Both are Proven Winners.

heat-resistant. A white-flowered selection, similar in other respects, is named 'Silverbush'. 'Blushing Beauty' (PPAF) has cream petals tipped in pink. Grow as an annual; give it full sun.

Succulents (principally *Echeveria* and *Sempervivum* sp.) Many succulent (fleshy-leafed) plants are adaptable to container growing. The species *Echeveria*, which includes the popular plants commonly called hen and chicks, is often used in strawberry jars along with other species that can tolerate dry soil. A much smaller plant, the red-flowered spiderweb or cobweb houseleek (*S. arachnoideum*) displays beautifully in trough gardens planted with other slow-growing species among imbedded stones. Hen and chicks is hardy only through zone 7, but the houseleeks will overwinter as far north as zone 5. Grow in well-drained soil in full sun.

Sutera or **tiny stars,** often called bacopa. This one will be virtually impossible to rename as *Sutera* because the name bacopa appears on so many plant labels. But bacopa is the name of native southern ditch plant, not the little-leafed South African native that is so popular in hanging baskets. Sutera or tiny stars is hard to classify, because even though it grows into low mounds, it does a good job of billowing over the rims of containers and covers the rims of hanging baskets. It has tiny, closely spaced leaves and dense plants covered with dime-sized white blossoms. Cultivars with light blue or pink flowers are available. Two of the best recently introduced cultivars are the white 'Snowstorm' (PPAF), by Proven Winners, and the red 'African Sunset'. Feed and water tiny stars often; grow in light shade as an annual. These dense plants demand excellent drainage to prevent decay during hot, humid weather.

Sweet flag (*Acorus gramineus*) Some of the best grasslike plants belong to this genus. They range in height from very low growing to 1½ feet. All like moist soil. One way to provide it is to make a mound of potting soil in a large saucer without a drainage hole. Set the plants on the mound where they can root into the wet layer, yet absorb oxygen from higher up in the profile. Try 'Ogon', with

The succulents such as hen and chicks and sedum are unsurpassed for small containers that can't be watered regularly. The crushed stones act as a mulch and keep soil from splashing out of the basin.

bright yellow leaves, and 'Variegatus', with white-edged green leaves. A dwarf, yellow-edged cultivar is also available. Full sun to light shade. Perennial through zone 6.

Wishbone flower (*Torenia* spp. and hybrids) For many years, torenia languished among also-rans in garden flowers, despite its ease of growth from seeds and resistance to heat and humidity. Its color range left much to be desired. Then the All-America Selections winner, 'Clown Mixed Colors', was introduced, bringing good pink, white, and blue shades to join the basic purple. The most recent introduction is a trailing torenia named 'Summer Wave Blue',

The trailing blue torenia or wishbone flower 'Summer Wave Blue' has blossoms twice as large as the current standard variety, 'Clown Mixed Colors'.

which has significantly larger flowers than 'Clown' in a lavender bicolor. Even though it will trail somewhat, it builds up to a height of nearly 1 foot before it begins to spill over the rim of pots. Since it is "fielders choice" on where to list it, I put it among the mound-shaped plants. By the way, the wishbone-shaped stamens are very visible on this cultivar, which make it a good "story" flower for children. Grow in full sun in the North, partial shade elsewhere. With rich soil and plenty of moisture, it will flourish in full sun in the South. Frost-tender. Usually grown as an annual.

Zinnia (*Zinnia* spp. and hybrids) Late-season mildew on zinnias has been the bane of generations of gardeners. Then, several years ago, seed companies began to promote the narrow-leafed *Z. angustifolia*. It has slim, closely spaced leaves and strong resistance to mildew, heat, and dryness. Now, they have brought down *Z. angustifolia* plants in size and festooned the plants with more blossoms. Three colors are available at this writing: white, golden, and the original wild yellow from Mexico. Next, to incorporate a broader range of colors, breeders apparently crossed *Z. angustifolia* with the large-flowered *Z. elegans* to come up with the All-America Award winners 'Profusion Orange' and 'Profusion Cherry' (deep rose-pink). Both are semidouble and resistant to mildew and to weather stresses. Burpee has a similar, but single-flowered line of six colors that they call 'Pinwheel'. They grow into narrow-leafed plants about 1 foot high and 2 feet across. Grow in full sun. Annual.

■ In a hot area, narrow-leafed zinnias, fan flower, white periwinkle, pentas, and marigolds nearly obscure their container.

Mound-Shaped Plants That Prefer Cool Summers

(Grow in Full Sun Unless Otherwise Noted.)

Ageratum or **floss flower** (*A. houstonianum*) Modern ageratum hybrids are uniformly compact and long-blooming. Other container plants are enhanced by the rich blue they provide. 'Blue Blazer', which grows to only 6 inches in height, is the smallest of the lot, but you won't go wrong with any of the many varieties offered. Pink and white varieties are also available, but they tend to look brown around the edges of the blossoms after flowering for a few weeks. A deep violet-blue color is available in the 'Hawaii' hybrids. The newer blue hybrids are fairly heat-resistant in the upper South but will stay in flower longer if given afternoon shade and are

deadheaded. Annual; grow in full sun to light shade.

Begonia, tuberous-rooted (*Begonia* hybrids) For years, the large-flowered, fully double hybrid 'Non-stop' bush-type begonias led the pack. Now, the same seed breeder, Benary, has introduced 'Ornament', an improved fully double hybrid. It comes in several brilliant colors that display beautifully against elaborate, very dark bronze leaves with green veins. The plants of 'Ornament' are dense and compact, less than 1 foot in height. Even in cool-summer areas, grow with afternoon shade or light shade all day long and in fertile, well-drained, organic soil. Water and feed the plants frequently. Frost-tender.

Begonia, wax (*Begonia semperflorens*) Yes, I know that wax begonias grow well in the South, but you should see them in

■ Sculpted pot planted with ivy, bacopa, Rieger begonias, and Hawaiian snowbush (*Breynia nivosa* 'Roseapicta').

hardiness zone 6 and north! These would be the leading flower for containers were they a bit more restrained in growth. In the North they grow fairly large, but in the long seasons of the South they can bush out to a width of 18 inches by the end of summer. It seems that every seed breeder has a "series" of fancifully named wax begonias, and they range from good to excellent. Most of the colors are in the pink, white, and red range. You have to turn to the tuberous begonias for a strong yellow. All wax begonia hybrids have glossy foliage in either green or burgundy shades. Generally, the larger the leaves, the more robust the plant. Typically, the bronze-leafed varieties will tolerate more heat than those with green foliage. Grow as an annual in full sun to light shade.

Black-eyed Susan (*Rudbeckia hirta*) Most varieties of black-eyed Susan are much too large for all except the largest containers. But little 'Toto' grows to only 10 inches tall and equally wide. Its yellow-gold daisy-type blossoms are surprisingly large for such small plants. It will bloom for several weeks in hardiness zone 6 and north, but bloom is limited to early summer further south. Makes a good substitute for dwarf marigolds. 'Viette's Little Suzy' developed at Andre Viette's nursery is more vigorous than 'Toto' and should be used only in large containers. Full sun to light shade. Annual.

Cabbage and **kale, ornamental** (*Brassica oleracea*) These are grown for their colorful foliage, not for their flowers. In cool-summer climates, ornamental cabbage and kale can be planted in the spring for several weeks of color before warm weather forces them to shoot up flowers and seed heads. However, the prime times for planting are late summer in the North and late fall in the South

■ The sides of the ancient wheelbarrow have rotted away, so the gardener set an old wooden box on the bed frame and filled it with pots of wax-leafed begonias.

and warm West. Grow these in individual 3-gallon pots for fall color, or set three plants in a 5-gallon basin. Keep cabbage worms under control with *Bacillus thuringiensis* biological insecticide and you will enjoy rich purple, pink, cream, and green color until killing frost. Genetically, there is little difference between the ornamental cabbages and ornamental kale. The cabbage varieties have entire leaves and relatively little fringing, whereas the kales can have either deeply curled and fringed, or deeply cut, lacy leaves. Even when plants are small, they show their colors. Don't rush the season and plant ornamental cabbage or kale before summer heat is behind you, or the plants may grow tall and

leggy. They are much prettier when they stay low and spread widely. Grow in full sun or light shade.

Catmint (*Nepeta faassenii*) Useful as a gray-leafed foliage plant in large concrete or hypertufa containers that will remain in the garden all winter. It is a hardy perennial and will need cutting back in the spring to renew the woody stems near the center. Catmint is a sister species of catnip, but has smaller, less furry leaves, and airy spangles of light lavender-blue flowers. Cats won't ravage its plants like they do those of catnip. Grow it in full sun.

Cobbity daisies and **dwarf marguerites** (*Argyranthemum frutescens* cultivars) Several of the recently introduced

Cobbity Daisies and Midgee Dwarf Marguerite Daisies are from Proven Winners. All have fairly compact plants and lots of daisy-form blossoms in pink, white, rose, yellow, and red shades. The Midgee cultivars mature at about 1 foot in height while Cobbity Daisies are somewhat taller. Reasonably heat-resistant, they stay in bloom longer

where summers are cool. Technically, these are short-lived perennials, hardy through zone 7, but are usually grown as annuals. Set containers in full sun or high shade.

Coral bells (*Heuchera* x *brizoides*) Hardy perennial coral bells come in several sizes, from compact plants that would fit in a quart jar to spreading, big-leafed cultivars like 'Palace Purple'. So you have to choose a cultivar that is in scale with the size of the container. You will have a great time choosing which to plant because so many new foliage colors are available, including those with silver cobweb variegations and warm-color edging. All have sprays of tiny reddish or white flowers that attract hummingbirds. Grow in moderate shade where summers are hot, and in either light or filtered shade in cool-summer areas.

Dahlia, dwarf (*D. pinnata*) A number of dahlia selections and hybrids mature at around 1 foot in height. 'Figaro' is one of the most compact. It has green foliage and comes in a great number of colors. 'Diablo' grows to about 15 inches and has purple-bronze foliage and mostly double flowers. In cool climates, dahlias will bloom all summer, especially if the spent blooms are deadheaded. Grow in full sun. Save the tubers in cool,

■ **Clay pot with cobbity daisies, false licorice, and 'Blackie' sweet potato.**

dry storage, and divide them for replanting the following spring.

Dianthus or Chinese pinks (*Dianthus chinensis*) Most of the breeding work among the many species of dianthus has been done in England, but some excellent cultivars have come out of California and Japanese seed companies. These cultivars are bunch-forming and grow into rather short, erect plants, with blossoms nearly 2 inches in diameter, either solid-colored or zoned. Some cultivars will live through the winter in zone 7 and south, and can be saved for replanting. None of the annual cultivars are strongly fragrant, but you can find many clove-scented choices among the perennial species of pinks. Among the annuals you can find cultivars with solid-

colored blossoms, bi-colored in zones, or bi-colors with a suffusion of the base color tinting the tips of the petals. I like the 'Telstar', 'Magic Charms', and 'Ideal' series of colors. Full sun to light shade.

English daisy (*Bellis perennis*) Beloved in Great Britain for bloom through the spring season, these are also grown for winter flowers in Florida and California, whenever or wherever nights are cool. They form plants no larger than a coffee mug, topped with fully double flowers on 6-inch stems. The 'Habanera' series developed by Benary has five colors and bi-colors in white, red, and rose shades. Full sun or light shade. These refined cultivars are not as hardy as the robust English daisies that naturalize in lawns in cool-summer areas.

■ **Dianthus, lobelia, coreopsis, and impatiens adorn this ancient, lichen-covered wheelbarrow.**

Ferns (various genera) Finding winter-hardy dwarf species or selections of ferns shouldn't be difficult, but you should select only the species that are naturally dwarf. The native dwarf ebony spleenwort will tolerate dryness and moderate shade. 'Crested Lady' fern is often used in dish gardens as a filler. Japanese painted fern grows fairly large but is often seen in large containers. Most everyone knows Boston fern, but it grows so large that it is most often grown alone in large containers and is brought indoors for the winter. Ferns help in mixed plantings by providing dependable green foils for flowering plants as they go in and out of bloom. Grow ferns in light to moderate shade. They like containers with a mulch of stones so they can root underneath them for moisture. Perennial.

Fuchsia (*Fuchsia* hybrids) Granted, some fuchsia cultivars trail nicely, but most grow into a loose, globe shape. I can't think of another flower with more intricately formed blossoms in more delicious shades of pink, white, crimson, and purple, with bi-colors galore. Even though they can't stand extremes of temperature and grow best in coastal California, gardeners who live where summers are hot plant fuchsias in containers for spring or fall color, and gardeners in the North plant for two months of summer bloom. When combining fuchsias with other flowers in large containers, the challenge is to find subdued colors that won't upstage the fuchsias. Look first at the lobelias, browallia, and dianthus; there you are most likely to find compatible kinds. Grow in light shade. Technically perennials, most fuchsias are grown as annuals, except in coastal parts of California.

Geranium (*Pelargonium* hybrids) Until recently, I would have had no misgivings about listing geraniums among the flowers that don't like summer heat. But my friends at Goldsmith Seeds sent me sample plants for 'Maverick'. They arrived in early June, nearly two months after we usually plant geraniums. I

promptly wrote back, "I'll plant them, but don't expect too much. They will burn out with the first hot weather." Well, they didn't. Shortly after planting they began forming whopping big clusters of red flowers on long stems. The hottest summer on record didn't faze them. They flowered without letup until our late August monsoon season blew in with heavy rains and high humidity. The plants were still vigorous, but finally quit blooming. I didn't have time to deadhead them or they might have gotten a second wind. Further north and west of my zone 7 garden, you can count on geraniums for all-summer color in containers, particularly if you deadhead them and give them an occasional shot of fertilizer—not a lot, or you'll have growthy plants and little bloom. Incidentally, the ivy-leafed geraniums are more sensitive to heat than the standard zonal types. The 'Martha Washington' group must have cool summers to bloom. Full sun. Grow as an annual.

Germander (*Teucrium chamaedrys*) You can use these small, compact, dark green, rather shrubby plants in many ways in containers, especially among stones. I've seen germander growing and doing well from northern Florida to Minneapolis, but it grows larger and blooms better in the North. It is a hardy

■ (top) These planters are salvaged from discarded dies used to make plastic wading pools; they are planted with ferns for growing in a shade house.

■ (middle) Asparagus fern (*Asparagus densiflorus* 'Myersii') and sweet alyssum, past bloom stage, thrive in a basin atop a shaded wall.

■ (bottom) Hanging basket of fuchsia 'Snowburner'.

perennial, evergreen or partially so in all locations. Its bloom span is short, only 2 or 3 weeks, but the small, rosy flowers are quite pretty. Give germander supplemental limestone except in the arid West. Full sun to light shade.

Grasses, ornamental dwarf cultivars The dwarf grasses mature at 1 foot or less in height and spread slowly. They make good foils for showier ornamentals. Try dwarf garter grass (*Phalaris arundinacea*) or dwarf fountain grass (*Pennisetum* x 'Little Bunny'). Other grasslike plants such as *Carex morrowii* 'Aureovariegata' and *Acorus* can serve the same purpose. Most gardeners treat them as annuals, not realizing that the sedges and

Acorus are fairly winter-hardy. Grow the grasses and sedges in full sun; *Acorus* can withstand light to moderate shade.

Heucherella Just a short time ago, it was a real feat to cross two different species. Now, they've crossed two different genera, *Heuchera* and *Tiarella,* to get some of the most exotic-looking, hardy perennial shade plants you will ever see. I can picture them growing among the flashy new perennials such as the Japanese painted ferns and *Pulmonaria* 'Excaliber'. (Yes, I know that's not how they spell the name of the sword, so let's get back to heucherellas.) Look for them in the Plant Delights catalog. You won't find a more up-to-date listing of the new heucheras, heucherellas, and other shade-loving plants, especially plants that will take the heat and humidity of the Southeast. Light to moderate shade.

Hostas See description under heat-tolerant, mounding plants. Actually, hostas grow well over much of the country, south to hardiness zone 9. Where winters are severe, most gardeners dump their containers of hostas in early fall and heel in the crowns by planting them in their garden. After the spring thaw the crowns can be dug up and replanted in containers that have been stored indoors for protection from freezing and thawing.

Lobelia, compact types (*L. erinus*) Breeders worked for years to develop lobelias that bunch up into compact, globe-shaped plants. Now they have them in several colors, and the little plants can be tucked in between larger ornamentals as fillers. The vegetatively propagated 'Compact Royal Jewels' reputedly blooms longer than seed-grown types where summers tend to be moderately warm. It has rich, deep-blue flowers with white centers. However, I've known the old favorite compact varieties such as the blue 'Crystal Palace', the cherry-red 'Rosamund', and the white 'Snowball' for many years and can't find fault with them. I only wish they were

■ Plants with inconspicuous flowers, such as this ornamental sedge (a denizen of moist places in the wild) are useful for adding foliage accents to collections of container plants. This sedge is at Heronswood Gardens, Bainbridge Island, Washington.

more heat-resistant. Grow in full sun. Annual.

Marigolds, dwarf French and **Gnome** or **Signet types** (*Tagetes patula* and *T. tenuifolia*) It was a toss-up between classifying the small marigolds as heat-resistant or as preferring cool weather. Actually, they grow very well in either cool or hot, humid climates but usually quit blooming or begin dying off in late August in the latter. I like the 'Janie' types for their small, globe-shaped plants and abundant bloom but find that the larger, more vigorous plants of 'Bonanza Bolero' withstand heat better. It won an All-America Selections award. If you wish to attract butterflies, plant the single-flowered dwarf variety, 'Disco Mixed

■ This South Carolina homeowner lost a large but hollow oak tree to a storm but gained an attractive planter. He filled the stump with soil and planted dwarf French marigolds.

Colors', also an AAS winner. I like the Signet types such as 'Lulu' and 'Tangerine Gem' as well; they have larger, more spreading plants than dwarf French marigolds but have tiny leaves and loads of small, single, edible flowers. Full sun. Annual.

Mint (*Mentha* cultivars) I often see the variegated cultivar 'Frosty Lace' mixed with other flowers in large hanging baskets, and it is lovely. It probably was selected out of pineapple mint for wavy, fringed leaves and uniform variegation and would rate only so-so for flavor. If I want culinary mint for sauces and drinks, I plant either peppermint or spearmint in 5-gallon containers where they can be fed and watered frequently. The plants should be dumped out at the coming of winter, heeled-in for protection, and divided the next spring before replanting in a container. Full sun to light shade. Hardy perennial.

Nasturtium (*Tropaeolum majus*) When visiting the production fields of Sahin Seeds in Holland, I saw a nasturtium variety that impressed me greatly. It is 'Empress of India', and the reason I can call up its image years later is that its foliage is dark, bronzy purple—unusual for a nasturtium. Its blossoms are large, velvety, and deep crimson. It isn't a new va-

A large "dish garden" of sweet potato 'Marguerita', Million Bells 'Cherry Red', Cape fuchsia (*Phygelius* 'Winchester Fanfare'), and mint 'Frosty Lace'.

riety, but has rather compact plants and should look wonderful in containers against plants with lighter-colored foliage such as 'Bergartten' sage. Full sun to light shade. Frost-tender.

Nemesia fruticans 'Compact Innocence' and 'Blue Bird' both PPAF, both Proven Winners. The name 'Compact Innocence' shows you what can happen when a rather rangy plant with a lovely name is shortened to a compact shape. Despite the clunky name, 'Compact Innocence' is a charming little plant with spires of miniature white blossoms and a dreamy scent. Its plants are globe-shaped and grow about 1 foot high. 'Blue Bird'

is semitrailing and, rather than being blue-flowered, has tiny blossoms of purple-blue. Grow as an annual in full sun to light shade.

Pansies and violas (*Viola* cultivars) Durable pansies bloom right through the winter in zone 7 and south. Further north, they are planted in early spring for bloom through July or August, when they are pulled out. Of all the scores of pansy colors and blends offered, my favorite is 'Antique Shades', an agreeable companion for many other cool-weather flowers in containers. The tiny violas called Johnny-jump-ups are perennial, but volunteer so readily from

■ **Australian or Tasmanian violet (*Viola hederacea*) makes a strong, trailing plant in pots but can become invasive if planted in a garden in moist soil.**

dropped seeds that thinning out is a yearly duty. Rock-garden specialists rely on them for spring color in troughs and sinks. Grow in full sun to light shade.

Scented geraniums (*Pelargonium* spp.) Grown more for their aromatic foliage than for their blossoms, scented geraniums come from many *Pelargonium* species, and in many foliage forms, colors, and fragrances. Some such as 'Rose Cinnamon' can grow too large for all but the largest containers, but several cultivars grow no more than a foot high and

half as wide from spring planting. If you grow them in well-drained soil, scented geraniums can withstand a lot of heat. In late summer, take tip cuttings, root them, and carry them over winter indoors in small pots. Full sun. Frost-tender.

Streptocarpella (*Streptocarpus saxorum*) You will be seeing more of these plants now that the cultivar 'Concord Blue' is becoming widely available. The small, furry, dark-green plants are rather lax and spill over the rims of hanging baskets. Blossoms like blue snapdragons with white markings are borne singly on slender stems all summer long. The faintest breath of a breeze sets them in motion. Grow in light to moderate shade. Frost-tender.

Swan River daisy 'Ultra' (*Brachycome* hybrid) PPAF by Proven Winners. For such a small, lacy-leafed plant, it withstands heat well, while performing beautifully where summers are cool. 'Ultra' has larger flowers than the species, and on shorter plants. Now the breeders at Benary have introduced a mixed-colors version, *Brachycome iberidifolia* 'Bravo', with blue, violet, and white colors, some with white rings around dark discs and others with yellow discs. The little globe-shaped plants grow only 8–10 inches high. Full sun. Annual.

Sweet alyssum (*Lobularia maritima*) You couldn't ask for a better or more

fragrant filler flower for containers than sweet alyssum. Plants of modern varieties seldom exceed 4 inches in height when grown in full sun and spread to about a foot across. The fine-leafed foliage is almost hidden by the many small blossoms. 'Snow Crystal', a Fleuroselect (European) winner, has the largest individual flowers of any, and its plants stand up against beating rains. The other colors of sweet alyssum are soft rose, lavender-pink, near-red, and rosy purple. There is no true pink. Sweet alyssum begins to look ragged during the dog days but either recovers when cool fall weather arrives or grows a second crop from dropped seeds. Full sun. Annual.

Thrift (*Armeria maritima*) Thrift comes close to being the ultimate "cushion plant." A hardy perennial, it forms small, nearly round, very dark green buns of narrow, grasslike leaves, about the size

■ Bamboo cachepot with streptocarpella 'Concord Blue'.

of a softball. Since I'm spouting sports equipment similes let me add that pink blooms the size of ping-pong balls show on short stems from early spring through early summer. In cool climates, the evergreen plants will remain attractive all

The two-tiered arrangement of blue pots enlivens this garden. Planted with verbena, lantana, sweet alyssum, and hen and chicks.

grow more than head-high. Some tall cultivars like 'Pretoria' or 'Bengal Tiger' have striped foliage, while others have dark purple leaves. All bloom the first summer from small plants or rhizomes, and all bloom for a long time despite heat and humidity. You may have to grow your cultivars alone in containers until you learn their blossom colors, before attempting to combine them with other flowers. In zone 7 and north, trim off the stalks, dump out the container, and store the rhizomes indoors to protect them from freezing. Grow in full sun or light shade with plenty of water.

Cape fuchsia (*Phygelius* x *rectus*) These are not fuchsias and actually look more like penstemons or foxgloves with their tall spikes of long, tubular blossoms and extended stamens. As yet little known in the U.S., the cape fuchsias have tall, slender plants up to 3 feet in height. Give them adequate water and good drainage in containers and they will bloom right through hot summer weather. In nature, they are shrubby perennials, hardy through about zone 7, and thus are suited to planting in large concrete or hypertufa containers that are left outdoors during the winter. Several cultivars are available, ranging in color from yellow through shades of pink and salmon. 'Winchester Fanfare' is perhaps the best-known cultivar, along with

summer. The variety 'Laucheana' ('Splendens') is early blooming and a favorite among growers of alpine and rock-garden species for hypertufa troughs and sinks. Full sun or light shade. Grow as an annual except in coastal California.

Erect, Rather Slim Plants, Moderately Resistant to Heat and Humidity

Canna (*Canna* cultivars) The foliage of cannas is large and bananalike, bold and often variegated. The challenge in finding cannas for containers is selecting ones that mature at 3 feet or less in height. Some of the common cultivars

'Salmon Leap' and 'Moonraker'. Light shade in the South, full sun in the North and cool coastal areas of the West.

Coleus, Sun-Tolerant (*Coleus* cultivars) These Coleus are worlds apart from the old-fashioned seed-grown, mixed-color coleus. They are vegetatively propagated to produce plants that are similar enough from plant to plant to be sold under cultivar names. They are foliage plants that come in bravura colors with fantastic markings, and which flower late and sparingly. Sun-tolerant coleus can be grown in full sun where summers are cool but prefer afternoon shade in warm-summer areas. Left to their own devices the plants would become rather bushy, but you can prune them to produce slim plants for the center of large containers. Cultivars come in two basic types: large-leafed and small-leafed. The ones with small leaves usually have comparatively small plants. Some garden centers offer as many as two dozen cultivars of sun-tolerant coleus. My favorite among them is the pinkish-buff 'Alabama Sunrise'. Frost-tender.

Daylilies (*Hemerocallis* hybrids and tetraploids) Daylilies are the leading hardy perennial for sunny gardens. They come in evergreen types for mild-winter areas and deciduous types for most of the country. The medium-height cultivars work best in containers but don't begin

■ (top) This big pot holds the chocolate-leaved sweet potato (*Ipomoea batatas* 'Blackie'), canna 'Pink Futurity', New Zealand flax (*Phormium tenax* 'Sunset Revert'), *Phygelius* sp. 'Salmon Leap', and *Clerodendrum* 'Minihassae Cream'.

■ (bottom) Blonde clay pot with chartreuse false licorice and sunfast coleus.

A fake marble basket with a verdigris finish holds small pots of geranium, spike, and trailing false licorice.

blooming until early summer. You might consider planting three different cultivars in a single container. Choose them for successive bloom, from early through late summer. You also might try combining yellow daylilies with purple heliotrope or *Verbena tenuisecta*. You may have to do some mixing and matching, but the right color combination could

be a winner! The compact, long-blooming daylilies such as 'Stella d' Oro' can be grown alone in 5-gallon containers. Full sun.

Dracaena or **Spike** (*D. marginata* and *D. sanderana*) The almost indispensable tall foliage plant for the center of large containers, frost-tender, tropical dracaena forms fountainlike plants when young, but develops erect, central stems with age. *D. marginata* has long, narrow, dark green, ribbonlike leaves edged with pink or purple. *D. sanderana* has wider green leaves striped with white. Despite their being typecast as indoor plants, the dracaenas do very well outdoors during summer weather. Both species can recover from drought and heat stress but stay in better condition if watered and fed frequently. Pot up your dracaenas and bring them indoors for the winter in zone 9 and north. Full sun or light shade.

Flowering tobacco or **nicotiana** (*N. sylvestris*) This is the old-fashioned annual, 3–4-feet-high nicotiana with fragrant white flowers that are best viewed in the evening. The basal foliage is bold and wide-spreading and requires a container of at least 10 gallons capacity. In windy areas the plants may need a sturdy bamboo stake to prevent the tall, slender plants from bending or breaking. The dwarf hybrids in the *Nicotiana* x *sanderae* group come in many colors that stay

A planting of heroic size is made possible by this 30-gallon tub: fan flower 'Blue Wonder', nicotiana, vinca vine, chartreuse false licorice, red pentas, and *Bidens* 'Golden Goddess'.

open all day but lack the powerful fragrance of *N. sylvestris.* Grow in full sun in the North, afternoon shade in hardiness zone 9 and south.

Gomphrena or **globe amaranth** (*Gomphrena haageana*) Of the three basic plant types in annual gomphrena, the only one with relatively tall, slender plants is a beautiful, long-flowering deep-red selection, 'Strawberry Fields'. It was selected from the original orange-flowered species. The blooms are marble-sized, tightly wrapped like clover buds, and carried on 18-inch, nearly leafless stems. You can also find small, globe-shaped plants in the dwarf selections from *G. globosa,* 'Buddy', and 'Cissy', which like *G. haageana* have extraordinary resistance to heat and dryness. Full sun.

■ *Zinnia angustifolia* (orange) and white *Gomphrena globosa* growing in pots sitting in a red coaster wagon.

Oxeye (*Heliopsis* sp.) I recently tried a new dwarf variegated heliopsis, 'Lo-raine Sunshine' from Blooms of Bressingham in Lapeer, Michigan. It bloomed in early July on plants 2 feet tall and wasn't fazed by hot, humid weather. The green and white foliage is every bit as beautiful as the yellow daisy blossoms. Of the dozens of cultivars of the many perennial species growing in containers around my garden, I considered this one the most handsome. I planted it in a large container along with a new red hot poker named 'Cobra', a dwarf yellow and green variegated Joseph's coat (*Alternanthera*) named 'Frizzy', and trailing varie-

gated vinca vine. It sounds like a crazy combination, but it worked!

Red hot poker (*Kniphofia uvaria*) 'Flamenco' is one of the hottest new tall flowers for large containers. An All-America Selections winner, it shoots up spikes to a height of 2–3 feet. Bloom comes in mid- to late summer from spring-planted potted plants; you don't have to wait two seasons for blooms. Closely packed tubular flowers crowd the spikes. They may be yellow, orange-red, or bi-colored, and the spikes change color as they age. The foliage is grasslike and arching. A moderately hardy perennial, *kniphofia* (sometimes called *Tritoma*) will perform best in concrete or hypertufa containers left outdoors during the winter. In hot, dry areas, you may wish to try the highly rated, orange-flowered 'Shining Scepter'. All the kniphofias are attractive to hummingbirds. Give them full sun.

Society garlic (*Tulbaghia violacea*) I especially like the variegated cultivar of this South African species. It has cream margins on its long, slim, arching, silvery-green leaves. All summer long, its leafless flower spikes are topped with clusters of lavender-pink flowers. All parts are faintly garlic-scented, but not offensively so. In zone 7 and north, store the bulbs in a dry place over winter and replant them in the spring. Full sun.

Surprise lilies or **hurricane lilies** (*Lycoris radiata*) These are not lilies, nor do they resemble them. They grow from bulbs that are hardy through zone 7. The plants develop and multiply slowly and do not like to be disturbed. They go through two cycles: vegetative (spring) and flowering (late summer). The 2-foot-tall bloom spikes are leafless and topped with ball-like clusters of bright red, tubular blossoms. I would plant surprise lily bulbs deep in a hypertufa trough or sink and overplant with *Sedum ternatum* and small cultivars of hen and chicks. Grow in full sun.

■ Red hot poker (*Kniphofia uvaria*) is a popular plant for containers with its tall flowering stalks; it needs excellent drainage.

Erect, Rather Slim Plants That Prefer Cool Summers

Celosia (*Celosia argentia,* Spicata group) The annual celosias are good hot-weather plants, but the fact is they stay in condition longer in zone 6 and north. The recently introduced 'Pink Candle', sometimes called wheat celosia for its grasslike leaves and slim heads, will draw admiration when three plants are set close together in the center of large containers. Its plants are tall—up to 3 feet in height—and slender, with wheatlike

■ **Purple salvia stands out against these pots of impatiens, false licorice (*Helichrysum petiolare* 'Petite'), Million Bells, thyme, sunfast coleus, scented geraniums, and dracaena.**

leaves and slender, two-toned pink spikes. If you plant the dwarf plume or crested celosias, be sure to deadhead the spent blossoms to encourage new blooms to form. Grow in full sun.

Salvia (*Salvia* spp.) Two kinds of salvia are especially adapted to planting in the center of containers: the blue mealycup salvia varieties from *S. farinacea,* and the All-America Selections award winner, 'Lady in Red', selected from the native *S. coccinea.* Both are quite heat-resistant, yet will give all-summer color in cool areas if set out as budded plants. You can also get white-flowered or bi-color (apricot-cream) varieties in *S. coccinea.* By the way, I planted red *S. splendens* alongside blue *S. farinacea* and red *S. coccinea.* Deer ate the *S. splendens* to the ground but ignored the other two! Blue salvia and *S. coccinea* are short-lived perennials and are treated as reseeding annuals in hardiness zone 7b and north. Full sun.

Snapdragon (*Antirrhinum majus*) Snaps are a favorite cool-weather flower in the South and West, and a good summer performer in the North. Individual plants have several stems, each of which is topped with a spectacular spike of ornate flowers. Over the years, a huge range of colors and bi-colors has been developed. You can buy them just as flower buds begin to open, and if you remove spent blossom spikes, new ones will form. The only problem with snaps as a tall flower is that commercial bedding plant producers focus on the short to medium-height varieties, which bloom early, and you may have to grow your own tall hybrids from seeds sown early indoors. Snaps often overwinter in hardiness zone 7 and south. Grow in full sun.

■ Cigar plant
(*Cuphea ignea*) in a
3-gallon pot at
Linden Plantation.

Woody Plants for Hot Summer Climates

(These Require Medium-Large to Large Containers.)

Cigar plant (*Cuphea ignea*) The plants of this subshrub *Cuphea* are less dense than those of Mexican heather (*C. hyssopifolia*), and the leaves take on a reddish tint late in the season. Even though the individual flowers are curious, they aren't large enough to make this a flashy plant. Look at them closely and you will see the similarity to a cigar in the white tip on the red tube, complete with dark, ringlike ashes. Usually grown alone in 3–5-gallon pots. Treat as an annual in zone 9 and north. Full sun.

Elderberry, variegated (*Sambucus nigra*) Common elderberry would grow far too large for containers, but the variegated cultivar 'Madonna' grows slowly enough for use as an accent plant in large containers. The foliage has such a large proportion of white to green that containers have to be given afternoon shade to avoid scorching leaf margins. It is amazing how this plant will draw your eye when backed up by dark green shrubs or foliage plants, or when planted in a shaded corner. Not reliably hardy north of zone 7.

Firecracker plant or **coral bush** (*Russelia equisetiformis*) These plants never fail to draw attention when they are in full bloom, which is much of the year.

A variegated flowering maple (*Abutilon* sp.) provides a great backdrop for sweet potato 'Blackie', petunia 'Purple Wave', a sunfast coleus cultivar, and two varieties of variegated *Plectranthus*.

The tubular flowers are brilliant orange-scarlet and draw hummingbirds, but the foliage is also extraordinary. Bright green and arching, the slender, leafless stems are round and multibranched. They look like scouring rush or horsetail, thus the species name. Grow with excellent drainage and beneath eaves in rainy areas to keep the plants on the dry side. The frost-tender plants can be overwintered indoors under lights. Full sun to light shade.

Flowering maple (*Abutilon* spp.) A frost-tender, erect shrub, usually with green, maplelike leaves, but sometimes spotted with cream. Can grow head-high where winters are mild. The large, pendent, bell-like flowers are showy, and come in yellow, orange, pink, and white shades. Plant breeders recently introduced dwarf, early-blooming cultivars with arching branches for sale in bloom in pots as gift plants. The blooms of all the cultivars attract hummingbirds. Full sun to light shade. Set the plants on posts so you can look up at the dangling blossoms.

Glory bush (*Tibouchina urvilleana*) A frost-tender, tropical shrub, often floppy in growth, with big, dark-purple, velvety blossoms, with reddish twigs and calyxes. Can be pruned to make it grow more

dense. Marginally hardy in zone 8, but stores quickly sell out of it in hardiness zones 6 and 7, where it is grown as an annual and sacrificed at the end of the season. Grow it in large containers in full sun.

Hawaiian snow bush (*Breynia nivosa*) The variety 'Roseapicta' is a showstopper. It looks like an erect, shrubby robinia or locust, but has green leaves mottled or zoned with pink and white. There is also a cultivar with dark purple leaves. I've seen it in Florida and California grown as singles or in trios in large containers, with a necklace of mounding and trailing plants to hide its

bare shanks. Native to Pacific islands and frost-tender, it can take high humidity and heat. Grow in full sun or shade.

Hibiscus, tropical (*H. rosa-sinensis*) A tender shrub/small tree, usually with dark-green, glossy foliage, but sometimes variegated. Comes in many blossom colors and forms, both single- and double-flowered. Usually sold as a single-stem specimen, but sometimes with multiple trunks. The blooms on tropical hibiscus come and go, depending on the fertility level in the container and the relative humidity of the air, but on balance will give you more color per plant than any other species. You can bond with your

■ **At the angle formed by intersecting walks, a raised bed is mulched with volcanic "red rock" and topped with containers of marigolds, petunias, verbenas, and Mexican heather.**

hibiscuses so tightly that you will find ways to pamper them through the winter indoors in zone 8 and north. In zones 9, 10, and 11, tropical hibiscuses are hardy through most winters. Full sun.

Mexican heather (*Cuphea hyssopifolia*) You probably have seen these small, dense, semihardy plants with tiny, glossy leaves and hundreds of small, purple-blue flowers. Not a true heather, they are very popular for growing in containers, as heat doesn't discourage blooming.

Mass marketers sell so many of them that the price per plant is usually quite reasonable. The plants grow to a height of 18 inches in hardiness zone 7, but a bit taller further south. Often planted alone in 3-gallon containers. Available also in pink- or white-flowered cultivars. Full sun to light shade. Frost-tender.

New Zealand flax (*Phormium tenax*) This New Zealand native is beginning to rival dracaena as a grasslike plant for the center of large containers. It has rather broad, lax, dagger-shaped leaves. When young, its plants grow into an attractive fountain shape. With age, they develop a stout central trunk. Several cultivars with different color variegations in the leaves are being marketed. More are available in Florida and California than elsewhere in the U.S. because the plants are frost-tender. Grow in full sun where summers are cool, in afternoon shade elsewhere.

Persian shield (*Strobilanthes dyeranus*) This frost-tender Burmese (Myanmar) plant successfully crossed over from a tropical houseplant to acceptance as a showy plant for outdoor containers. It has large leaves, up to 8 inches in length, iridescent silver above, purple beneath, and toothed along the margins. It has 1½-inch violet flowers in large spikes, but the extravagant foliage is its real strength. Will reach up to 3 feet in height when grown as an annual in 15-gallon and larger containers or very large hanging baskets. Needs a collar of mounding and trailing plants to cover its lanky legs. Grow in light to moderate shade and away from strong winds.

Skyflower (*Duranta erecta*) Blue-flowered shrubs are much in demand. This one is native to south Florida and has naturalized in protected places along the Gulf Coast, where it grows into a small tree. Elsewhere, it is grown as a shrub and protected through the winter. It has beautiful blue-green foliage and spectacular sprays of 1/2-inch diameter flowers in white, lavender-blue, or purple, followed by waxy yellow fruits. There is a variegated cultivar but it is hard to find. Garden centers as far north as zone 7 are beginning to stock skyflower because it grows quite well in containers of 10-gallons size and up, and gains in size rather slowly. With faithful feeding and watering it will stay in color all summer. Grow in full sun.

Climbing or Clambering Vines
(These Require Large Containers and Trellises.)

Black-eyed Susan vine or **clock vine** (*Thunbergia alata*) Grown as an annual over much of the country. In areas of the West that are nearly frost-free the plants can grow to considerable size, but over most of the country they will reach no more than 3 or 4 feet in height, suiting them to containers of 7–10-gallons capacity. The furry foliage is nothing special, rather light green and angular, but the blossoms are extraordinary: large, flaring, deep yellow, with jet-black throats. A tropical thunbergia with large, navy blue blossoms, *T. battiscombei,* can be grown as an annual in northern locations if given a sunny site, protected from wind. It is often seen in hanging baskets. Full sun or light shade. Frost-tender.

Firecracker vine and candy corn vine (*Manettia cordifolia* and *M. inflata*) I lost the label on a plant of firecracker vine, *M. cordifolia,* and made up the name hummingbird vine, because the hummers love its dark-red, tubular flowers. My plant has survived several zone 7 winters, dying to the ground, but sending up slender, glossy-leafed, twining stems to a height of 5 feet by summer's end. Candy-corn vine (love that name) grows much like firecracker vine, and its blossoms are similar, except for being a lighter orange-red and having yellow tips. Neither species seems fazed by heat, humidity, or dryness, but the vines look better if watered regularly. These vines are just the right size for training up one of those western red-cedar trellises so common in garden centers. Difficult to find; you may have to order plants by mail. Grow in full sun or light shade.

Mandevilla (*Mandevilla* x *amabilis*) This showy, large-leafed tropical vine began to move out of botanical gardens into home landscapes during the '70s. The pink-flowered cultivar 'Alice du Pont' led the market for some time but is now being supplanted by the darker-flowered 'Red Riding Hood', which can be grown as a bush. Karen Park Jennings of Park Seeds likes the cultivars 'Janelle' and 'Leah'. The bush forms were once known as *Dipladenia,* but this is not a valid scientific name. *M. sanderi* 'My Fair Lady' is a recently introduced climber with white blossoms flushed with pink. The mandevillas are tender but can be cut back to near the ground and stored indoors in a near-dormant state during the winter. Full sun.

Plumbago or **Cape Plumbago** (*P. auriculata*) One of the most beautiful, blue-flowered vines. In zone 7 and north, plumbago is grown as an annual, and used as bushy specimen plants in pots. Where winters are mild, the plants grow much taller and are tied to supports. The clustered flowers look a bit like phlox. In addition to the common light blue, a darker blue cultivar, 'Royal Cape', is available, as is a white-flowered selection. Full sun or light shade.

Spanish flag (*Ipomoea lobata*) formerly *Mina lobata*. Annual in hardiness zone 8 and north, native to Mexico. It is a high-climbing vine grown as an annual over much of the country, and although in the same genus as the morning glories, doesn't resemble them closely. Large, one-sided heads of multiple, tubular flowers, yellow with darker

■ The modern bush *Mandevilla sanderi* 'Scarlet Pimpernel'.

markings, appear in midsummer and continue through fall. A real attention-getter, and attractive to hummingbirds. Plants of Spanish flag are hard to find and you may have to grow them from seeds planted in pots after frost danger is past. Full sun.

Ten

Reports from U.S. and Canadian Experts in Container Plants

In North America, the first persons to grow and evaluate new plants are usually the horticulturists at botanical gardens and public gardens such as theme parks. Their gardens belong to a worldwide network where plant explorers send species that are new to cultivation, or where plant breeders submit new cultivars for evaluation. Now, aided by the Internet, these gardens can communicate and share information much more expeditiously than in the past.

You might think that such programs would hasten the obsolesence of old but good cultivars. Not so. There will always be room for tried-and-true cultivars, but it is incumbent on public gardens to promote superior cultivars and previously unknown species that prove adaptable to their specific climate and soil by two or three seasons of evaluation.

Trials of ornamentals in containers are an important activity at public gardens, not only because they use so many containers in their landscaping, but also because of the high degree of interest in

container gardening by hobby gardeners.

The following lists of choice container plants were submitted by horticulturists at public gardens. In most reports, the flowers and foliage plants are arranged alphabetically by botanical name, but the generally accepted common name, where one exists, will be given as well. You will notice a high degree of overlap, with certain flowers appearing on many lists. It speaks to the wide adaptability of many flowers to container culture and to the sharing of information between public gardens. Note, also, the interest in secondary attractions in container plants such as fragrance and their ability to draw butterflies and hummingbirds.

Reports were received from horticulturists at the following gardens:

Huntsville–Madison County Botanical Garden, Alabama
Lewis Ginter Botanical Garden, Richmond, Virginia

Norfolk Botanical Gardens, Norfolk, Virginia

The Butchart Gardens, Victoria, British Columbia, Canada

Boerner Botanical Gardens, Hales Corners, Wisconsin

Missouri Botanical Garden, St. Louis, Missouri

Harry P. Leu Gardens, Orlando, Florida

Longwood Gardens, Kennett Square, Pennsylvania

Brookside Gardens, Wheaton, Maryland

Botanica, The Wichita Gardens, Kansas

Callaway Gardens, Pine Mountain, Georgia

Desert Botanical Garden, Phoenix, Arizona

Fort Worth Botanical Garden, Fort Worth, Texas

Disney's Horticulture, Walt Disney World, Inc., Lake Buena Vista, Florida

Riverbanks Zoo and Botanical Garden, Columbia, South Carolina

Cleveland Botanical Garden, Cleveland, Ohio

Huntsville–Madison County Botanical Garden, Alabama

Several years ago, I lectured on container plants at the Huntsville–Madison County (Alabama) Botanical Garden and was especially pleased to receive this list of species and cultivars that perform well for them in containers. It was prepared by Garden Curator Mike Gibson, and Greenhouse Production Manager Sherry Carroll. They emphasized considering the drought tolerance of plants because of the difficulty of keeping container soils moist during their hot summer months.

Acorus gramineus. Cultivars of this sturdy, grasslike plant come in cream or white on green variegations. Prefers light shade all day but will thrive with afternoon shade. A durable plant, drought-tolerant, but will stay in better condition if a good level of soil moisture is maintained.

Arctium lappa, burdock. Some gardeners consider this coarse-leafed plant a weed, but we find it is a fast-growing, durable source of heart-shaped foliage. We don't let it go to seed. Our herbarists have uses for it. Watch out for insects; some species will feed on burdock.

Arenaria montana, sandwort. Prefers sandy loam or a soilless mix such as Ball No. 2. Looks good all year, with clumps of fine-textured foliage. It will trail over pot rims like classical grape clusters. Brilliant white flowers like *Nierembergia* come in the spring. It needs exposure to cold to flower but is very heat-tolerant with no major insect or disease problems. Our only losses have been from failure to water on time. Favors a site with sun most of the day. Easy to grow from seeds or vegetative divisions.

Carex muskingumensis, palm sedge. A wispy, graceful, grasslike plant, native to North

America. Forms tufts of light green foliage. The cultivar 'Ohme' is lightly variegated. Suited to light to moderately shaded areas or where shaded in the afternoon.

Evolvulus pilosus, blue daze. Considered frost-tender, this somewhat woody trailer has proved hardy outside here for several years. It produces a continuous show of silvery-green foliage and small but numerous blue flowers, spring through fall. Watch out for rabbit damage in early spring; they like to nibble the young plants.

Heuchera americana, alumroot. We particularly like the hybrids from Dan Helms, such as 'Cascade Dawn'. It has maple-leaf foliage in mosaics of gray, green, purple, and silver. Will tolerate sun but the margins of leaves tend to scorch during hot weather. The flowers are nothing special, so we pinch off all but a few, which provide vertical interest. A good companion for hostas in containers for shaded areas.

Lantana camara, bush lantana. One of our summer mainstays. A heat-tolerant sun-lover that attracts butterflies. In autumn, we salvage well-grown specimens from our display beds, overwinter them in greenhouses, and train them into tree forms for next year's containers. 'New Gold' is a favorite here.

Lantana montevidensis, trailing lantana. Another dependable plant for sunny locations. We like the cultivar 'Lavender Weeping' and a prostrate white-flowered form. They have thin stems that we weave together and train to stand upright as multitrunk "standards."

Pennisetum alopecuroides 'Rubra', purple fountain grass. We like to plant this 2–4-foot-tall grass behind clumps of yellow lantana for dramatic contrast. This ornamental grass arches nicely and is heat- and drought-tolerant.

Ruellia brittoniana 'Katie'. Its low-growing clumps of dark green foliage, like that of peach trees, are topped with clusters of lavender-purple, petunialike blossoms. This cultivar has been hardy ouside here through several winters. Very heat-resistant.

Sedum bithynicum. Native to Greece. It grows into a mat of fine-textured, aqua-blue, mostly evergreen foliage. Looks good trailing over pot edges and as a filler between larger plants. Tolerant to drought and strong sunlight. You can propagate it easily by pressing small lengths of stems and leaves into the soil; they will root in place.

Sedum sexangulare. Like *S. bithynicum,* except with dark green foliage that holds up well to winter cold.

Zinnia angustifolia (formerly *Z. linearis*), 'Classic Gold' and 'Tropic Snow'. Good, spreading plants for sunny locations. Although mildew can affect the young seedlings during wet spring weather, they are trouble free once they become established and toughen up. Resistant to heat and drought.

Also noteworthy as container plants are:

Artemisia (wormwood) cultivars
Buxus sempervirens 'Kingsville', boxwood
Coleus, sun-tolerant cultivars
Gomphrena globosa, globe amaranth
Hedera (ivy) cultivars, used as trailers over pot rims
Petunia hybrids. A wide variety of petunias perform well for us in full sun.
Pentas lanceolata, star cluster flower

Petroselinum crispum, parsley. Grow in light to moderate shade as a dark green filler plant.

Portulaca grandiflora, rose moss or portulaca

Scaveola aemula, fan flower

Thymophylla tenuiloba, Dahlberg daisy

Thymus species, thyme, various species and cultivars. Grow as wispy filler plants.

Torenia fournieri, wishbone flower

Verbena hybrids, perennials

Lewis Ginter Botanical Garden, Richmond, Virginia

Among the advantages that accrue from years of work in home and commercial horticulture are the delightful people I chance to work with along the way. One of these is Holly Shimizu, managing director of the Lewis Ginter Botanical Garden in Richmond, Virginia. I first met Holly and her husband, Osamu, back when she managed the herb garden at the National Arboretum in Washington, D.C. I have shared *Victory Garden* taping sessions with Holly, and my wife and I have enjoyed their company on lecture cruises on board the American Queen paddle-wheel steamboat from New Orleans to Memphis.

The Lewis Ginter Botanical Garden is admired for its spectacular displays of seasonal flowers and container plants, so I am especially pleased to share their list of preferred container plants with you.

Only neat and nonaggressive cultivars that stand up to heat and humidity appear on their list:

Sun-Loving Cultivars

Alternanthera dentata 'Rubiginosa'. A very beautiful plant with rich purple foliage. Grows upright but can be pruned to shape.

Alternanthera ficoidea 'Aurea Nana'. The alternantheras are also known as Joseph's coat. This compact cultivar matures into a mounded form with green and gold markings on its foliage.

Capsicum annuum 'Jigsaw'. We like this showy ornamental pepper for its purple, green, and white foliage, and bullet-shaped purple fruits. Other cultivars with green fruits that turn yellow and red are also useful in containers. We tuck trailing plants of other species beneath the spreading branches of the umbrella-form pepper plants.

Pelargoniums, scented. Scented geraniums are actually in the genus *Pelargonium* and are not truly geraniums. We grow many cultivars for their distinctive foliage and aromas. Their flowers are nothing special, but the plants are so durable and undemanding that we mix them with showy flowers in containers. The fragrant leaves are usually cut or lobed into fanciful shapes and may be silvery-green, green and gold variegated, or zoned in mahogany, cream, and green.

Pennisetum setaceum 'Rubrum', purple fountain grass. It would be hard to find a better plant for the center of large containers. This purple-green ornamental grass grows to about 2 1/2 feet in height and arches outward. By midsummer, bristly, purple flower heads like squirrel tails appear and gradually mature seeds. Colorful flowers show up attractively against the long, dark leaves of this grass.

Pentas lanceolata, star cluster flower. The pentas, both the dwarf and standard-height cultivars, are in bloom when we set them in containers after spring frost danger is past, and they never let up until fall frost. We use the tall cultivars for height in the center of large containers and the dwarf types for their mounded shape. Pentas attract numerous butterflies.

Plectranthus argentatus. This is a robust, silvery-green foliage plant, with fleshy, downy leaves half the size of your hand. It grows upright and is often used in the center of large containers. Its tiny blue flowers are insignificant.

Plectranthus, other species. Many plectranthus cultivars with green or green and cream or green and gold leaves grow well in containers. Usually sold in 4–6-inch pots, they will have assumed their characteristic form—either trailing, mounded, or upright—by the time you purchase them.

Tradescantia (Setcreasea) pallida 'Purpurea'. Also known as purple heart, this is one tough, durable, undemanding foliage plant. It can endure short periods of drought and recover without apparent damage. It has long, slim, canoe-shaped, purple leaves that drape over the rims of pots.

Plumbago auriculata 'Escapade', cape leadwort. We grow this cultivar for its deep blue clusters of blossoms that keep coming for months. Plumbago starts off as a mound of foliage with short tendrils that by late summer will trail over the rims of pots, or soften edgings along garden walks. It displays nicely when planted alone in pots of 10-gallon size.

Lantana camara and *L. montevidensis* cultivars. These are bush and spreading types, respectively, but so much hybridization has been done recently that the distinction between the two is blurring. All show lots of color from spring through the first heavy fall frost and are a magnet for butterflies. A tender perennial, lantana usually winterkills here.

Senecio cineraria, 'Dusty Miller'. This genus contains some of the most attractive silvery-white foliage plants, which are sold as 'Dusty Miller'. The leaves of most cultivars are deeply cut and lacy, but some have oval leaves with wavy, ruffled edges. The plants grow rather slowly; we value them for mixing among flowering plants in containers. Mature plants have sprays of yellow blossoms in late summer, but you seldom see blossoms where summers are short.

Vinca major, large-leafed vinca vine. Both the green-leafed and green and white variegated versions of this vine trail attractively and stand up well to extremes of heat and humidity. One of the best plants for trailing straight down from hanging baskets.

Zinnia angustifolia, narrow-leafed zinnia. This native of Mexican drylands is one of the most heat- and humidity-resistant flowers we grow. It blooms all summer in shades of yellow, orange, and white. The blossoms are about the size of a silver dollar and are very abundant. The plants start off mound-shaped but by midsummer will billow over the rims of containers.

Container Plants for Shaded Sites

Abutilon x *hybridum* 'Bella', flowering maple.
You can buy cultivars that grow into
erect, tree-form plants, 4–5 feet high by
the end of the season, or low, spreading
types with cream-spotted foliage. A wide
range of blossom colors is available, in single or double forms. The bell-shaped
blossoms hang face down, but acrobatic
hummingbirds have developed strategies
for extracting nectar from them. With frequent watering and feeding, abutilon
plants will grow in full sun but can get by
with less care in afternoon shade or light
shade all day.

Coleus. We grow many of the numerous sun-
tolerant coleus cultivars in containers and
a few of the older fancy-leafed cultivars
that require more shade. The sun-tolerant
cultivars are slow to form flower stalks,
thus require little deadheading. The older
standard coleus varieties are grown from
seeds and show more color variation than
the vegetatively propagated sun-tolerant
types. We give standard coleus afternoon
shade or light shade all day. Neither type
is drought-tolerant; they require consis-
tently moist soil.

Ipomoea batatas. You often see the ornamental
sweet potatoes grown in full sun, but their
large leaves on trailing vines transpire so
much water that we prefer to grow them
where they are lightly shaded all day. We
plant 'Blackie' (chocolate), 'Marguerita'
(chartreuse), and 'Pink Frost' (green, pink,
and white variegated). 'Blackie' and 'Marguerita' are robust, and we combine them
with fast-growing flowers, but 'Pink Frost'
grows slowly and can be combined with
small plants.

Norfolk Botanical Garden, Norfolk, Virginia

I've spoken at this beautiful garden several times and never fail to be impressed
by their gardens, both in the ground and
in containers. Their proximity to the
broad sound separating Norfolk from
Newport News moderates the climate,
taking the edge off both summer high
and winter low temperatures. Michael A.
Andruczyk, their curator of plant collections, sent this list of choice container
plants that grow well for them:

Argyranthemum 'Chelsea Girl'. A tough plant
with beautiful, lacy green foliage for full
to part sun. Daisylike blossoms. Doesn't
bloom for us during the hottest days of
summer but does bloom well during cool
spring and fall weather.

Calamagrostis x *acutiflora* 'Karl Foerster',
feather reed grass. A tall, erect, red-bronze
grass that turns buff in the fall. Good central plant for establishing a vertical dimension in containers. Likes to be grown on
the dry side in a sunny site.

Coleus (renamed *Solenostemon*) 'Pineapple',
'Solar Sunrise', 'Alabama Sunset'. These
sun-tolerant cultivars have good, tough,
bright foliage in full sun or light shade.
They require regular watering.

Colocasia esculenta 'Black Magic' and other
cultivars. Common names of the edible
species include cocoyam, taro, and
dasheen. Good central focal plant with
large, purple-chocolate, dramatic leaves.
Grow in sun or light to moderate shade

with regular watering and feeding

Cordyline australis cultivars, New Zealand cabbage tree. Available in several purple, green, cream, and copper variegations, all fancifully named. Broad, arching, grasslike leaves. Bold central focal plant that lends a textural accent to large containers. Full sun to light shade.

Hibiscus acetosella 'Red Shield'. We grow this one for its burgundy foliage; its flowers are insignificant. Develops rapidly and is best grown alone in a large container as a specimen plant. Yet, with pruning, it can serve as a tall focal plant in a mixed container. Full sun to light shade.

Ipomoea batatas, ornamental sweet potato. 'Blackie' and 'Marguerita' are strong, vigorous trailers for a range of exposures from full sun to light shade. 'Tricolor' has nice colors but lacks the vigor of the former cultivars.

Pelargonium 'Balcon Series'. Garden geranium. A great, tough plant that blooms well for us in sun and shade. Cascades over the rims of pots.

Petunia x hybrida 'Wave' color series. Good plant for cascading from hanging baskets or over the rims of pots. Needs regular watering and spot checks for bud worm infestation. Grow in full sun or light shade.

Setcreasea pallida (*Tradescantia pallida*), purple heart. Good foliage/textural accent with linear, purple leaves. For full sun to moderate shade.

Trachycarpus fortunei, fan palm or Chinese windmill palm. Good as an erect, central plant in large containers and to enrich the blend of textures in mixed plantings.

Wedelia trilobata. A good, tough, trailing foliage plant with nice yellow flowers. Full sun to light shade.

The Butchart Gardens, Victoria, British Columbia, Canada

When people ask me the most beautiful public garden I've ever visited, I must answer, "For its size, The Butchart Gardens." Situated in a one-time quarry, Butchart is not a large garden, but its floral impact is so powerful that your senses seem overloaded. In operation since 1904, The Butchart Gardens brings huge crowds to Vancouver Island, just west of Vancouver, B.C. Rick Los, their director of horticulture, commented, "Although our containers are generally low maintenance, they require occasional deadheading. Regular feeding and adequate watering will provide a continuous display of color, with bloom from spring to autumn in our temperate coastal climate."

Mr. Los added, "We are continually experimenting with different combinations in containers at different times of the year to give our patio areas more interest and a fresh look. The positive reactions of visitors inspire us to continue to stretch our creativity." He and Cindy Hamilton, their horticulturist in charge of container plantings, suggested some seasonal combinations, including:

For color during the winter in mild climates, full-sun exposure

Carex morrowii 'Fisher', sedge (mounding)
Cornus alba 'Siberica', red-barked dogwood (erect)
Corylus avellana 'Contorta', Harry Lauder's walking stick (erect)
Euphorbia amygdaloides 'Purpurea', purple wood spurge (erect)
Hedera helix, ivy (trailing)
Nandina domestica, heavenly bamboo (erect)
Pieris japonica 'Variegata', Japanese pieris (mounded)
Polystichum munitum, holly fern (mounded)
Viburnum tinus 'Variegata', variegated laurustinus (erect)

For a tropical look during the summer, large containers in full sun

Canna x *generalis* 'Tropicana', canna (erect)
Grevillea robusta, orange-flowered silky oak (erect, tree-form)
Ipomoea batatas 'Blackie', ornamental sweet potato (trailing)
Ipomoea batatas 'Chartreuse', ornamental sweet potato (trailing)
Pelargonium, ivy-leaved, geranium (trailing)
Ricinus communis, castor bean (erect, branching)

For a simple, low-maintenance, summer-color container, full sun or afternoon shade

Amaranthus caudatus, love-lies-bleeding (erect/drooping tassels)
Rudbeckia 'Indian Summer', black-eyed Susan (erect)

For summer color in a large container in light shade

Fatsia japonica 'Moseri', glossy-leaved paper plant (erect)
Hedera canariensis 'Variegata', variegated ivy (trailing)
Helichrysum petiolare 'Limelight', false licorice (trailing)
Hosta 'Golden Prayers' (mounding)
Hosta 'Undulata' (mounding)
Tradescantia pallida 'Purpurea' (trailing)

For a whimsical combination in a large container, part sun to moderate shade, summer

Browallia speciosa 'Heavenly Bells', bush violet (spreading)
Fuchsia 'Checkerboard' (trained to tree form)
Helichrysum petiolare 'Limelight', false licorice (trailing)
Lamium maculatum 'Beacon Silver', lamium (trailing)

Boerner Botanical Gardens, Hales Corners, Wisconsin

I've visited this spacious spread of specialized gardens and displays several times. Years ago, my visits were to confer with John Voight, who was recognized as one of the top experts in the country on annual flowers. Later, I returned to tape TV shows for *The Victory Garden* and with Melinda Myers, a network TV personality, and to promote the Plant a Row for the Hungry program of the Garden Writers Association of America.

Southeastern Wisconsin is a great place to garden, and the experts at Boerner Botanical have to stretch to meet the demand for gardening information and displays of the latest and best in cultivars. My friend and director of Boerner Botanical Gardens, Laurie M. Albano, sent this list of species and cultivars, prepared by staff horticulturists, that grow well in containers at their gardens:

Abutilon hybridum 'Luteus', (flowering maple). Not a true maple, but a tropical, heavy-blooming shrub that stays in flower all year long, outdoors during the summer and indoors during the winter. Its bell-shaped flowers are deep yellow. Can be trained into a standard (tree) form. Likes full sun here.

Alpinia zerumbet 'Variegata', variegated shell ginger. This tropical plant has very decorative green leaves streaked with bright yellow. The foliage shoots emerge upright, then arch outwards. Our plants seldom flower as they do where summers are longer and warmer, but the beautiful foliage is reason enough to grow it. Will grow in full sun or light shade.

Asparagus densiflorus 'Sprengeri', asparagus fern. Fine-textured, bright green foliage on mounded plants that billow over the rims of pots. We treat it as a frost-tender perennial here. Grows well in sun (if kept moist) or in light to moderate shade.

Brugmansia arborea, synonym *B. versicolor,* angel's trumpet. In shrub form or trained to single stem, this tropical plant with its large, fragrant, elegantly pendulous, salmon-pink blossoms grows in full sun to light shade.

Cordyline australis 'Baueri'. An erect, spiky, tropical plant grown for its burgundy foliage. Related and somewhat similar to *Dracaena* 'Spike'. It grows well for us in a number of situations, from full sun to moderate shade all day.

Diascia 'Ruby Field', twinspur. We grow this tender perennial as an annual. It produces masses of small, salmon-pink flowers on mounded plants 12–18 inches in height. Makes a good filler flower. Grow in full sun.

Fuchsia x *hybrida* 'Gartenmeister Bonstedt'. This fuschia has an upright habit of growth with long, slender, pendulous coral flowers in bloom continuously through spring, summer, and fall. The bronze-green foliage sets off the bronze-red stems nicely. We grow it successfully in either full sun or moderate shade. The tubular flowers attract hummingbirds.

Helichrysum petiolare 'Petite', white false licorice. Good filler plant for containers, with tiny, fuzzy white leaves and an open growth habit. Will trail over pot rims by midsummer. Tolerates heat and somewhat dry conditions. We treat it as a tender perennial and grow it in full sun.

Hibiscus rosa-sinensis 'Brilliant'. This tropical plant blooms all summer with large, single, bright red, showy flowers up to 6 inches across. Using it trained to a tree form allows room for underplanting in a large container. It can tolerate high temperatures; needs full sun.

Ipomoea batatas 'Blackie', sweet potato vine. Robust plants with burgundy-black, lobed leaves and a trailing habit of growth. Tender perennial, best grown in full sun.

Lantana 'New Gold', trailing lantana. Clusters of deep yellow flowers on trailing plants that bloom profusely in hot weather. We treat lantana as a tender perennial and grow it in full sun.

Melianthus major, African honeybush. At our northern latitude, this tender, evergreen shrub may produce a maroon flower spike, but not until late summer. We grow it mostly for its large, textured, blue-green, deeply divided leaves, and in a variety of locations, from full sun to light shade. Very attractive when contrasted with dark colors.

Pennisetum setaceum 'Rubrum', red fountain grass. The common name for this ornamental grass comes from its erect, arching stems, which suggest a fountain of water. Both its foliage and seed spikes are burgundy-colored from a young age. We use it as a centerpiece in large containers and treat it as a tender perennial. Best grown in full sun.

Plectranthus argentatus, quicksilver plant. A big container is needed to accommodate the large plants of this quick-growing tender perennial. It is an erect, branching plant with fleshy stems and velvety silver leaves. Best grown in full sun.

Salvia chamaedryoides, blue oak sage. A dainty plant with small, attractive gray leaves and short spikes of bright blue flowers. Grows into a mounded form. We treat this species as a tender perennial and grow it in full sun.

Salvia sinaloensis, sinaloa sage. A spectacular plant, with bronzy foliage and intense, deep blue flowers and a mounded habit of growth. We treat it as a tender perennial and grow it in full sun.

Scaevola aemula 'New Wonder', fan flower. We find this cultivar very useful for its dense, trailing growth, covered with lavender-blue flowers all summer. Although it will tolerate heat and occasional dryness, it performs best in well-drained soil with diligent watering and feeding. Tender perennial, best grown in full sun.

Strobilanthes dyeranus, Persian shield. Tropical-looking plant with dark green leaves overlaid with metallic silver and lavender markings. Makes a great centerpiece for a large container. Erect growth with limber branches. Tender perennial that grows well in sun (if kept moist) or in light shade.

Sutera cordata 'Snowflake', synonym *Bacopa monnieri,* water hyssop. This rather recently introduced plant has become almost essential for hanging baskets and as a filler plant in pots. The low-growing plants produce long cascades of trailing, emerald foliage dotted with tiny white flowers. Grows well in full sun (if kept moist) or in light to moderate shade.

Torenia 'Summer Wave', vining wishbone flower. Light blue flowers with darker blue markings on vigorous plants. They start out with a mounded shape but by midsummer billow over the rims of pots and trail down. Best grown with afternoon shade or with light to moderate shade all day long. Frost tender. Requires faithful watering.

Tradescantia pallida, synonym *Setcreasea purpurea,* purple heart. Deep purple foliage and tiny, heart-shaped, lavender-pink flowers in the axils of leaves. A trailing, heat-resistant, tender perennial. Grows well in full sun or light shade.

Tulipa 'Passionale', triumph tulip. No container is more spectacular than one chock full of early-blooming tulips. Triumph tulips bloom reliably when "forced" by prechilling the bulbs; its blossoms are a lovely lilac-purple with a cream colored base. We bring the potted bulbs out of cold storage into light and heat to bloom in late April and early May, and protect the containers from late frosts. Place in full sun or light shade.

Verbena 'Temari Bright Pink', trailing verbena. Branching, spreading plants with a trailing habit and clusters of fragrant pink blooms. Heat-resistant. Best grown in full sun.

Missouri Botanical Garden, St. Louis, Missouri

I'm a University of Missouri alumnus, and I have always felt a special fondness for this world-renowned garden and its illustrious staff. I was flattered when it appeared that they had put a committee together to respond to my request for information on container plants, but then it dawned on me that the individuals were inputting from different facilities in the garden where they utilize container plants. I am grateful to Shirley A. Dommer, June Hutson, Jon Sweeney, and Cathy Pauley for their collective contribution to this book. Note: St. Louis may belong in hardiness zone 6 (perhaps zone 5 at higher elevations) but its summers are more like what you would expect in zone 7. Here are the species and cultivars that grow well for them:

Acalypha wilkesiana 'Kona Coast', copperleaf
Breynia nivosa 'Roseapicta', snow bush
Canna 'Tropical Rose', canna lily
Capsicum 'Treasure's Red', ornamental pepper
Catharanthus roseus 'Mediterranean Series', periwinkle
Evolvulus pilosus 'Hawaiian Blue Eyes'
Gomphrena 'Strawberry Fields'
Gomphrena globosa 'Buddy Purple'
Ipomoea batatas 'Marguerita' and 'Ace of Spades'
Lantana montevidensis, trailing lantana
Nierembergia caerulea 'Mont Blanc', cupflower
Origanum 'Kent's Beauty', ornamental oregano
Panicum virgatum 'Heavy Metal', blue switch grass
Portulaca 'Giant Bicolor Radiance', rose moss
Scaevola aemula 'Blue Wonder', fan flower
Solenostemon 'Alabama Sunset' and 'Trailing Duck's Foot', sun-tolerant coleus
Torenia 'Summer Wave', wishbone flower
Tradescantia pallida, purple heart
Zinnia angustifolia, narrow-leaf zinnia

The Missouri Botanical Garden horticulturists added, "Most of these plants can be combined in containers. They are heat- and humidity-resistant. All have neat, nonaggressive growth habits. We grow them in full sun."

Harry P. Leu Gardens, Orlando, Florida

Orlando is surrounded by great theme parks with splendid gardens. But Orlando residents also rely on a close-in, municipal garden for up-to-date information both on cultivars that will grow well in their zone 9 climate and on cultural methods for their diverse soil types. The Harry P. Leu Gardens doesn't aspire to be a classic botanical garden, but rather concentrates on floral displays and a strong outreach program.

Helen A. BeVier, horticulture manager, and Martin Haux, who are in charge of Leu Gardens' displays of annuals and containers, had this to say about container plants: "Like all gardeners, we use both annuals and perennials in our containers, but we thought the following list was representative of species and cultivars that grow well in containers in our Central Florida climate. It includes some plants that are seldom seen further north."

Abutilon x *hybridum* 'Dwarf Red', Chinese lantern. A dwarf "flowering maple" with an abundance of pendent, bell-like, red-orange flowers year-round. Easy to care for; not damaged by light frosts. Needs light to moderate shade. Keep the soil moist and fertilize monthly. Draws hummingbirds.

Adenium obesum, desert rose. Grow with afternoon shade during summer months but move the container to full sun when the weather turns cool. This slow-growing succulent has spectacular flowers throughout the year. Feed monthly and water regularly. It makes a great container plant but won't tolerate much frost.

Agave americana, century plant. Best grown alone in a large terra-cotta container where passers-by won't be pierced by the sharp tips on the fleshy leaves. Requires full sun but no care at all. May take years to send up a flower stalk and once it does, the plant dies.

Anthurium andraeanum hybrids, flamingo flower, tailflower. Among our favorite cultivars are 'Lady Anne', 'Kingston', 'Cotton Candy', 'Red Hot', and 'Bubble Gum'. A tropical plant for shaded outdoor sites. Looks good in containers of mixed ornamentals or grown by itself. Flowers twelve months of the year and always looks good, if kept moist and protected from strong winds, especially during winter months.

Brugsmansia x *candida,* angel's trumpet. This plant is poisonous, so we grow it where children can't get to it. The cultivars 'Double White', 'Ecuador Pink', 'Cypress Gardens', and 'Charles Grimaldi' grow well here in large containers. All of them have spectacular, pendent flowers, especially fragrant at night. The trumpets on some cultivars are white; on others they are yellow or golden-orange. Strong grower with light needs for fertilizer and water.

Chamaerops humilis, European fan palm. Full sun or part shade. A tough, disease-resistant, cold-hardy plant for year-round displays. Slow growth and easy care makes this palm a must for the beginner. Drought-tolerant and perfectly adapted to our local climate.

Cordyline terminalis, ti plant. There are a number of cultivars of this plant. Visitors to our garden particularly like 'Tequesta', 'Pink Sherbet', 'Red Sister', and 'Bolero'. An erect-growing, tropical foliage plant with colorful leaves year-round. It grows at a moderate rate and needs afternoon shade to avoid parching of leaf margins. A nice plant for mixed containers.

Heliconia stricta 'Bucky'. A semidwarf, summer-flowering tropical plant with brilliant, spectacular flower bracts as large as your hand. Needs light to moderate shade and lots of water and fertilizer.

Howea forsterana, kentia palm. A palm for deep shade. It must be protected from frost. Keep the soil in its container moist and fertilize regularly. Old specimens are very ornamental but pricey. It looks great as a solitary plant in a container.

Hyophorbe lagenicaulis, bottle palm. Another palm that is best grown alone. It grows very slowly and usually has only 4–5 fronds at any given time. Becomes highly ornamental with age. Tolerates no frost and prefers sun or part shade. A choice plant for collectors!

Morus alba 'Unryu', contorted white mulberry. Highly ornamental shrub/tree that drops its leaves in the fall, exposing the zigzag stems. Rarely grown, but it makes a good specimen plant grown in a large container by itself. Give it full sun and lots of water.

Nolina recurvata (formerly *Beaucarnea recurvata*), ponytail, elephant foot tree. An all-time favorite for containers. This palmlike plant has a swollen base with rough bark. It grows slowly, is drought-tolerant, and requires little maintenance. No collection of container plants for Central Florida should be without this reliable performer.

Portulacaria afra, elephant bush. Will take full sun or light shade. It is a slow grower that has a rather bizarre appearance at maturity. We like it because it requires little maintenance, little fertilizer, and no extra water. We protect these plants when a hard frost is predicted.

Wisteria sinensis, Chinese wisteria. We grow this into a tree form by training a branch up a stake, topping, then clipping it several times a year to the desired shape. Frost-hardy; will grow in full sun or light shade. Needs frequent watering and fertilizing. Deciduous. Its grapelike clusters of flowers come out early in the spring, before the leaves show.

Longwood Gardens, Kennett Square, Pennsylvania

This is a world-class garden which, with its proximity to Philadelphia, hosts nearly a million visitors a year, many of them gardeners from all corners of the globe. Longwood stages a flower show every day, keyed to seasonal bloom and holidays. At any one time about fifty students in horticulture study at Longwood. One of them, Jennifer Brown, who is training to become a professional gardener, interviewed the other gardeners at Longwood and came up with this consensus report on cultivars that grow well in containers. All the plants listed are tender perennials that Longwood grows as annuals.

Begonia sutherlandii. A beautiful cascading begonia with small orange flowers on medium green foliage. Use it to trail from hanging baskets in light to moderate shade.

Beta vulgaris var. *flavescens,* Swiss chard. Although usually grown as a vegetable,

Swiss chard combines beautifully with flowers in mixed containers. It comes in several foliage colors (red, white, yellow, pink), some with contrasting midribs. The upright leaves are crumpled and somewhat cupped. Use it for containers in full sun to add an unusual touch.

Brugmansia cultivars, angel's trumpet. Great, pendent, fragrant flowers, especially good for evening gardens. Plant these fast-growing plants in large containers.

Canna 'Pretoria' or 'Minerva'. We grow these two cultivars for their bold, coarse-textured, variegated (striped) foliage, and large, bright blossoms. We grow other canna cultivars as well, including the modern dwarf types that grow no taller than 3 feet. A broad range of blossom colors is available, with either green or purple foliage. Best grown in full sun and fed frequently. Otherwise, cannas require little care.

Ipomoea batatas 'Blackie' and 'Marguerita', ornamental sweet potato. Great foliage colors (deep purple and chartreuse, respectively) add a trailing accent to containers. The bold foliage gives a tropical look.

Phormium tenax 'Purpureum', New Zealand flax. This plant has purple-green leaves somewhat like the familiar *Dracaena*, except wider and longer. It is a great plant for adding a special texture to a setting. Very effective when grown by itself in a container. Even though the plant is erect, its long leaves arch in a fountain form. Grow in full sun; avoid overwatering.

Plectranthus amboinicus (green and white variegated form). Tough, fleshy plant that combines well in chartreuse color schemes. It has long, limber branches and felty leaves. This heavy feeder grows best in full sun.

Plectranthus madagascariensis. This imposing name tells you that the species hails from Madagascar. It has evolved into different varieties. This trailing variety has variegated foliage in contrasting bright white and green. Grow in either full sun or part shade.

Salvia mexicana. This plant has an upright form and light green leaves. From mid-summer on, it is adorned with spikes of clear blue/purple flowers. Grow in full sun or light shade.

Setcreasea pallida 'Purple Heart'. A rugged plant for full sun. Vibrant purple, trailing foliage with tiny pink flowers throughout the summer.

Strobilanthes dyeranus, Persian shield. Unusual in appearance, this large, exotic-looking plant has great purple/green/silver foliage. Grow it in full sun. Pest free.

Brookside Gardens, Wheaton, Maryland

Brookside Gardens serves the greater Washington, D.C., area and is in hardiness zone 6. Angela Clelan reported for their horticulturists in response to my query on plants that grow well in containers. All the species and cultivars listed are frost-tender perennials grown as annuals, except those especially noted.

Abutilon hybrids, flowering maple. The plant form can be upright to pendulous, depending on the cultivar. Grows best in part shade; draws hummingbirds.

Alternanthera dentata, "Rubiginosa', Joseph's

coat. Low-growing plants that fill in between other kinds in mixed plantings and trail over the rims of pots. We grow the cultivar with deep red foliage, in full sun to part shade.

Anisodontea x *hypomandarum,* African mallow. Upright subshrub that can be easily trained into a tree or standard form. It has loads of bright pink, open-faced flowers. Blooms all summer.

Agastache cultivars 'Blue Fortune' and 'Tutti-fruiti' were selected from the native American species *A. foeniculum* and *A. cana,* respectively. These tough, hardy plants grow upright with flowers in spikes and attract hummingbirds and butterflies. Use as erect plants for the center of large containers.

Breynia nivosa 'Roseapicta', snow bush. Erect plants, woody at the base, with beautiful green, white, and pink coloration when plants are exposed to bright light. Grow in well-drained soil in full sun.

Canna cultivars. We grow 'Tropicana' for the beautiful dark coloration of its foliage and its large flowers. It has comparatively short plants and is nonaggressive. 'Lucifer' grows somewhat taller and has green foliage and flame-colored flowers. Both grow erect and are great for adding height to large containers. Grow in full sun.

Coleus, sun-tolerant. This race of vegetatively propagated coleus has recently come forward as a major plant for sun or shade. Cultivars come in a broad range of colors and variegations and in upright or trailing plant forms.

Cuphea hyssopifolia 'Allyson', Mexican heather. Dainty, lavender flowers on dense, dark green, mounded plants. Drought-tolerant; thrives in full sun.

Cupressus macrocarpa 'Goldcrest'. A beautiful, erect, columnar conifer with golden foliage that wafts a lemon scent when touched. Grow in full sun. Frost-tender in this part of Maryland but can be protected through the winter in a cool, sunny room or greenhouse.

Datura wrightii 'The Black' (formerly *D. metel*). A very showy angel's trumpet with glossy, dark-purple flowers. Grows upright; blooms persist despite heat and humidity. Grow in full sun in a large container.

Fuchsia x *hybrida* 'Mrs. J. D. Frederick'. One of the best plants for hanging baskets or for trailing over the rims of containers. Young plants are mounded but soon send out short, trailing branches. Will bloom dependably in light shade or with afternoon shade, if fed and watered regularly.

Hamelia patens, firebush. Bushy, upright subshrub with orange-red, tubular flowers that attract hummingbirds and butterflies. Grows best in full sun. Thrives despite heat and humidity.

Heliotropium arborescens, heliotrope. Mounded, very dark green plants with rumpled, coarse-textured foliage and flat sprays of purple flowers. Pleasant, distinct fragrance. Attracts the evening-flying "hummingbird moths."

Ipomoea batatas 'Marguerita', chartreuse sweet potato. We use it as a trailing plant in large containers. It is vigorous and resistant to heat and humidity.

Lavandula x 'Goodwin Creek', lavender. A particularly attractive lavender with upright silvery-gray plants that bloom all summer. Can be combined with other flowering plants in containers. Grow in full sun with well-drained soil.

Mandevilla x *amabilis* 'Yellow' and *M. sanderi* 'Little Red Riding Hood' are less aggressive than common forms of mandevilla or dipladenia. The short vines can be trailed

over the rims of large containers or hanging baskets or supported by short trellises.
Grow in full sun.

Phormium tenax, New Zealand flax. Upright
plants with long, arching leaves that are
limber, not stiff. You can chose a cultivar
with variegations that please you, from
somber purple and green to brighter
stripes, to blend or contrast with mounding and trailing plants in mixed containers. Makes a good specimen plant when
grown alone.

Pennisetum setaceum 'Rubrum', purple fountain grass. Good, erect, central plant for
large containers. Easy to grow in full sun
or part shade. Annual.

Plectranthus argentatus. Large, upright foliage
plants with limber branches that weave
among other flowers in mixed containers.
The silver leaves look good with flowering
plants. Drought-tolerant; grow in full sun.

Salvia greggii, Texas or autumn sage. Erect,
branching bushes are covered with small
blossoms that resemble those of garden
sage. Drought-tolerant. Grow in full sun.
Attracts hummingbirds. Available in white,
crimson, yellow, violet, and pink cultivars.

Scaevola aemula 'Petite Wonder', 'Outback
Fan', fan flower. These lavender-blue-
flowered trailing plants thrive in heat and
full sun. They mix well with other flowers
in containers.

Strobilanthes dyeranus, Persian shield. The flexible branches of these bold, upright, tropical foliage plants descend and can be
woven among other flowers in mixed
containers. The large purple leaves have a
silvery sheen. Grow in full or half-day sun.

Verbena x *hybrida,* 'Old Royal' and 'Quartz'
color series. These fast-growing, spreading
plants stay low, bloom all summer, and
will trail attractively. Grow in full sun.
They can be cut back if they overgrow

their containers and will regrow quickly if
fed and watered regularly.

Zinnia elegans x *Z. angustifolia* 'Profusion
Cherry' and 'Profusion Orange'. We first
used these All-America award-winning
annuals for the 1999 growing season and
were very impressed. The mounding
plants stay low, cover their spent blossoms
with new foliage, and are resistant to
drought and humidity.

Ms. Clelan reports that in addition to
their seasonal containers, they also grow
certain cold-hardy conifers year-round
in large containers:

Juniperus conferta 'Blue Pacific' or 'Blue Star'.
Both have a trailing habit of growth and
blue-green foliage.

Juniperus horizontalis 'Golden Carpet' or
'Mother Lode'. Both stay low and spreading and have greenish-gold foliage.

Picea glauca, 'Alberta Blue', dwarf Alberta
spruce. Very dense and compact. Grows
upright into a conical form.

Sciadopitys verticillata, Japanese umbrella pine.
Handsome, upright, slow-growing tree,
with dark, glossy green needles in whorls.

Botanica, The Wichita Gardens, Kansas

In late summer 1999, I gave the keynote
address at the Central District of the
American Rose Society at Botanica. I
had never before visited this beautifully
designed garden and didn't know what
to expect. To my considerable surprise
and delight (Wichita is, of course, way
north of where I live), I saw many famil-

iar southern plants growing in containers. Turns out that while their summers are a month shorter than ours, they are every bit as warm, and tropicals and half-hardy perennials thrive. Pat McKernan sent me this list of their best performers:

Acalypha wilkesiana, copperleaf. An upright, shrublike, tropical plant with large, colorful leaves. Heat resistant; grow in full sun.

Agastache 'Heather Queen'. No common name. Developed from native American prairie species. Upright growth, heat-resistant, continuous bloom if dead-headed. Grow in full sun.

Aptenia cordifolia, ice plant. A very heat-resistant succulent plant for full sun to part shade. It blooms continuously during the summer and trails over the rim of containers. Easily propagated from cuttings.

Capsicum annuum, ornamental pepper. We like the cultivars 'Medusa', with compact growth and yellow, orange, and red fruit, and 'Jigsaw' with upright growth, purple fruit, and white/purple variegated foliage. Fruits of 'Jigsaw' are very hot. Both are heat-resistant, with 'Jigsaw' holding a slight edge in performance during very hot weather. Grow in full sun.

Centratherum punctatum, Brazilian button bush. Upright grower, very heat-resistant. Small, purple blossoms like shaving brushes show all summer long. Grow in full sun to partial shade.

Cuphea hyssopifolia, Mexican heather. Mounded shape, heat-resistant, with continuous bloom during the summer. Makes a great low-growing border in gardens in the ground. Site containers in full sun to part shade.

Duranta erecta, sky flower or pigeon berry. Strikingly beautiful, blue-flowered shrub that can be overwintered in a greenhouse. Heat-resistant, continuous bloom. Grow in full sun. Native to South Florida and the tropics.

Evolvulus glomeratus, blue daze. Continuous show of small, blue blossoms against trailing, gray-green foliage. Heat-resistant in full sun or part shade.

Heliotropium arborescens, heliotrope. Upright grower that blooms continuously if spent flowers are removed. Heat-resistant, grow in full sun to light shade. The purple flowers are very fragrant.

Ipomoea batatas, ornamental sweet potato. We grow 'Ace of Spades', 'Blackie', 'Marguerita', and 'Tricolor' in full sun for variety in foliage color. All trail attractively and are very heat-resistant. Easily propagated from cuttings.

Lantana camara (bush type) and *L. montevidensis* (trailing type). These two distinct species and the hybrids between them are very heat-resistant and bloom all summer, through extremes of heat and humidity. Drought-tolerant; grow in full sun. Butterfly flower.

Nierembergia caerulea 'Purple Robe' and 'Mont Blanc' (white), cupflower. These small plants are surprisingly sturdy and bloom from spring through fall. By midsummer they will trail over the rims of containers or from hanging baskets. We grow them in full sun.

Pennisetum setaceum 'Atrosanguineum', purple fountain grass. Few plants make better focal points for the center of large containers. The long, arching leaves and the bristly flower and seed heads are purple. Heat-resistant; grow in full sun.

Petunia x *hybrida* 'Purple Wave'. Low growing and trailing, 'Purple Wave' weaves among other more erect kinds planted with it in mixed containers. It blooms continuously in full sun to part shade and is somewhat heat-resistant. Needs well-drained soil and is susceptible to damage by bud-worms.

Plectranthus sp. All species of *Plectranthus* are heat-resistant and virtually problem-free at Botanica. The mint-leaved Swedish ivy has comparatively small, fragrant leaves and a trailing growth habit. The silvery-gray *P. argentatus* grows upright to 3 feet and can be pruned to encourage dense growth. It has large, fuzzy leaves. All are easily propagated from cuttings.

Rhynchelytrum nerviglume 'Pink Crystals', ruby grass. An unusual container plant with tall, upright growth and striking pink plumes. Heat-resistant; grow in full sun.

Scaevola aemula, fan flower. Heat-resistant and will stay in good condition if planted in well-drained soil and fed and watered regularly. Continuous show of small, one-sided, lavender-blue blossoms. Full sun to part shade.

Thymophylla tenuiloba, Dahlberg daisy. Small, trailing plants with lacy foliage and yellow flowers all summer. Somewhat heat-resistant if grown in well-drained soil.

Turnera ulmifolia, Brazilian buttercup. Upright growth, heat-resistant. All summer, the yellow blossoms contrast attractively against the deep green foliage. Full sun to light shade.

Verbena 'Imagination', perennial verbena. A reliable source of all-summer color, resistant to heat and occasional periods of dry soil. Strong-growing trailer. Butterfly plant.

Zinnia angustifolia (*Z. linearis*), narrow-leafed zinnia. Short, bushy plants are covered with small yellow, orange, or white daisy-like blossoms from late spring on. Resistant to heat, occasional dryness, and powdery mildew. Grow in full sun.

Wedelia trilobata, Indian runner. Little-known in this area, Indian runner is a fast-growing, trailing tropical with yellow-orange flowers. Will bloom continuously if fed and watered frequently. Grow in full sun.

Callaway Gardens, Pine Mountain, Georgia

From my days on *The Victory Garden* (PBS), I know about every corner of the many gardens scattered around this 2,500-acre resort. Thus, I know the importance they place on container plants, especially for maintaining spots of color where they can't grow gardens in the ground. Helen Phillips, who is curator of Victory Garden South, sent this list. She added, "We use so many different species and cultivars for seasonal color in containers that it was difficult to pare down the list of really good ones. These flowers on this list work like plow horses!"

Dendranthema pacificum. This plant holds up well through the summer. Its textural, silver-edged leaves contrast well with other plants in mixed containers. By fall, the clustered yellow buttons of blooms become a focal point within containers. We use it for mounded plants in pots sited in full sun.

Buxus 'Graham Blandy'. We pot up this

tightly columnar boxwood when the plants are about 2 feet in height and use it for vertical accents in planters of mixed herbs. Grown in full sun, this boxwood is like a sentinel on duty! Since it is slow-growing, it can be tapped out of the pot and set into fresh soil to begin each new growing season, year after year. (Many small, slow-growing evergreen shrubs could be used in a similar manner.)

Coleus 'Summer Sunrise'. In a large planter in full sun, the richly colored foliage of this sun-tolerant coleus blends beautifully with other flowers. It grows upright, but bushes out to take up a lot of space. Visitors to our garden exclaim over this cultivar.

Duranta erecta, yellow dew drops. One of the many names for this blue-flowered tropical, "yellow dew drops" comes from the waxy yellow fruits that follow the flowers. From midsummer on, the shrublike plants are decorated with both flowers and fruit.

Duranta loves full sun and needs only a trailing companion plant to complete a memorable container.

Hedera helix 'Gold Heart', variegated English ivy. In part shade, the gold-centered foliage of this ivy really stands out when combined with the narrow foliage of *Liriope* (lilyturf) and goldfish plant, *Aeschynanthus* sp. It trails over the edge of containers and needs no attention the entire summer except watering and occasional feeding.

Ipomoea batatas 'Blackie', 'Marguerita', and 'Tricolor', ornamental sweet potato. We use these three cultivars in many containers in our garden. They like full sun and don't seem to mind when we pinch off the tips of runners that grow too long.

Ophiopogon planiscapus 'Nigrescens', black mondo grass. The near-black foliage of this cultivar can add a wispy accent to containers of mixed flowers. It requires little care other than occasional feeding and regular watering. Grow in full sun. We recently used it around the base of a topiary chicken that we grew in a pot. The black mondo grass became the nest!

Pelargonium 'Snowflake', variegated scented geranium. The lovely green and white variegated leaves of this cultivar feel like velvet and when touched scent the air with the fragrance of roses. The plants are erect, but some branches will grow long enough to billow gracefully over the rims of pots. You can prune the plants as needed to keep them in bounds. Grow in full sun.

Plectranthus argentatus. Sometimes erroneously called Brazilian coleus, this useful plant has no generally accepted common name. Its felty, silvery-gray leaves can soften any combination of plants in mixed containers. Even with pinching the branch tips for dense growth, the plants can grow to a height of 3 feet and thus should be planted in a large container. Grow in full sun.

Plumbago auriculata, plumbago. The clear sky blue of its bloom clusters continues for about 3 months. Though it is technically a vine, we grow it as a tall, rather lax shrub in the center of containers for vertical dimension. We grow it in full sun and don't trim or prune it.

Salvia officinalis 'Tricolor', tricolor garden sage. The purple, green, and white variegated foliage of this plant make it a handsome partner for many other flowers in containers. Full sun keeps the colors clear and bright. It needs no pinching and has no pests!

Zinnia 'Profusion Orange'. At a height of only 12 inches, this unbelievable bloomer fits well in containers of mixed flowers. Its bright orange flowers with a single layer of petals keep on coming with little deadheading. It is drought-tolerant, stays in an attractive mounded form, and covers its faded blooms with new foliage.

Desert Botanical Garden, Phoenix, Arizona

My slide set on "Landscaping with Container Plants" opens with an image from the Desert Botanical Garden that never fails to excite favorable comments. It's a slide of a large container planted with several species of cacti and placed in the corner of a low stucco wall. It is only one of many containers featured at this heavily visited public garden.

Kirti Mathura, a horticulturist at the Desert Botanical Garden, submitted this list of species and cultivars that grow well for them. Understandably, the emphasis in container plants at the Desert Botanical Garden is on drought-resistant kinds. The species and cultivars on the list that follows perform well under their conditions of very hot, dry summers and short, rather mild winters. Thus, they would probably grow well in containers in southern New Mexico, west Texas, and in low-elevation gardens in Colorado, Utah, Nevada, and Southern California if protected from frost. They would probably also thrive if grown in fairly fast-draining soil under an overhang in the southeastern U.S. but would have to be sheltered in a greenhouse during the winter. You might have trouble finding some of these plants through other than mail-order sources specializing in desert-adapted plants.

Fairly Drought-Tolerant Succulents

Many agaves make wonderful container plants. Here are just two:

Agave macroacantha, an attractive plant whose blue-green leaves with dark tips contrast nicely with all-green plants. Grows best here when given morning sun and light shade in the afternoon.

A. vilmoriniana. Its soft-tipped, supple leaves make it the most "friendly" of the agaves, some of which are armed and dangerous. It grows fast to its mature height of 4–5 feet and adapts to different light conditions.

Aloe spp. Most aloe species do very well in containers, with shorter clumping types reaching 1–2 feet in height, and non-clumping types reaching several feet with age. Most prefer filtered sunlight all day or afternoon shade.

Euphorbia resinifera has a nice, thick-stemmed clumping habit and reaches about 1–1½ feet. Afternoon shade is best but can withstand full sun. Be careful about watering during the winter, as wet soil, when the temperature is low, can rot roots.

Gasteria spp. Succulents with clumping habit, many with interesting leaf color and/or foliage texture. Shows a great range of heights between species, from a few inches at maturity to 1 1/2 feet. Give them filtered sunlight all day or afternoon shade. The small, tubular blossoms attract hummingbirds.

Portulacaria afra. Its sprawling growth is great for large pots or planter boxes; the branches spill nicely over the sides of containers. The plants are sizeable, reaching 2–3 feet in height at maturity. With a big pot and watchful watering these can be grown in full sun, but to be on the safe side give them afternoon shade.

Sarcostemma viminale. Its pendulous, jointed branches adapt to large hanging baskets or pots hung on a wall or fence. At maturity, plants can reach 1–2 feet in height. Small, fragrant, white blossoms appear mostly during fall or spring. Grows best in filtered sunlight or afternoon shade.

Sansevieria spp. This is the durable "houseplant" species grown indoors where winters are severe. The species vary greatly in leaf color, variegation, and shape, and the clumps can grow from 6 inches to 3 feet tall, depending on the species. The fragrance of their greenish-white blossoms is especially noticeable in the evening. Grow in filtered sunlight or afternoon shade.

Drought-Tolerant Herbaceous Plants

Thymophylla (Dyssodia) pentacheata. Rather small plants that provide wonderful color when planted near the rims of large pots. They bloom for a long time during the summer and can be cut back periodically to stimulate reblooming. Grow best with morning sun and afternoon shade but could take full sun if given a little more water.

Muhlenbergia spp. These are ornamental grasses, most of which grow well in large pots in full sun or afternoon shade. Several bloom attractively with the coming of the fall season.

M. capillaris. Morning or afternoon sun backlights the misty, pinkish-red blooms to produce a spectacular effect, particularly when in bloom. Reaches about 3 feet in height at maturity.

M. dumosa. Plant where you can admire the great bamboo-looking stems. They arch into big arcs that sway gracefully in the wind. Grows to about 4 feet in height.

Origanum spp. Both the edible and ornamental oreganos grow well here. They need large pots to permit full growth and either full sun or afternoon shade.

Rosmarinus officinalis. Pretty much any of the cultivated rosemarys, upright or prostrate, do well here in containers. They grow quite large and eventually need huge pots. Grow in full sun. An excellent nectar source for bees.

Adapted, But Less Drought-Tolerant Species

With regular watering, these herbaceous or woody species grow well in containers here:

Laurus nobilis, European bay tree. This is the bay tree grown for seasoning. It makes a lovely, rather slow-growing, dark green shrub with glossy leaves year-round. Will stay in peak condition if grown in large containers, shifted up every few years, fed and watered regularly, and given morning sun and afternoon shade. Eventually, it grows too large for containers here and has to be planted in the ground.

Pelargonium spp., scented geraniums. We mix scented geraniums of the smaller sorts among flowering plants in large containers or grow the massive species alone as specimen plants. Place them beside a garden walk where you will brush against them and release the fragrance from their foliage.

Plectranthus amboinicus. This one looks great in large containers where it can sprawl over the rims and "weave" among other plants. It has thick, felty, green and creamy-white leaves. Very frost-tender. Grows best in filtered sunlight or morning sun.

This is just a sampling of the many kinds of plants that grow well in containers in our gardens. The peak seasons for viewing plants of all kinds here are spring (February–April) and fall (October–December).

Fort Worth Botanic Garden, Fort Worth, Texas

Rob Bauereisen sent me this list of plants that grow well in their rather strenuous climate at Fort Worth. Their summers are usually hot, quite dry, and windy, which can stress container plants growing in the open in full sun. Their winters are rather mild, but extremely changeable, which is hard on evergreen plants.

Allamanda cathartica, allamanda. This fast-growing, woody, tropical climber can grow to a height of 15 feet. Throughout the summer it produces large, yellow, trumpet-shaped blossoms up to 6 inches across that last but a day. They attract butterflies. Position the container next to a sturdy post or an arbor that can support the heavy vine, and try combining it with mandevilla. You may need to control aphids, and if you carry the vine over winter you may need to cut it back in the spring to increase flowering growth. Grow in full sun and fertilize regularly with water-soluble fertilizers.

Brassica oleracea acephala, flowering or ornamental kale. Cool-season plant for color in late fall and winter. Available in shades of rose, purple, white, and green and in a variety of foliage forms. Can be killed by severe cold and shoots up flower spikes with the lengthening of days in the spring. Looks best when 3–5 plants of the same variety are grouped in a large container. Don't plant during warm fall weather, or the plants might grow leggy. Plants grown in full sun color up the best. Grow in well-drained soils and fertilize regularly. The foliage is edible, so use non-toxic biological insecticides to control aphids and caterpillars.

Chlorophytum comosum, spider plant. The wild, green-leafed variety can be invasive in mild winter areas, but the many forms with cream or yellow-striped leaves are less aggressive and more attractive. Use it for foliage effects in hanging baskets and free-standing containers. Too much sun can damage spider plants, and you may have to grub out the little plantlets that detach from the long stems and take root in the ground. Easy to propagate and to care for. Grow in light to moderate shade.

Citrus sp., citrus. Edible lemons, limes, oranges, grapefruit, and others can be grown in containers that can be protected during freezing weather. The small-plant kumquat and calamondin varieties are especially popular for containers. All have glossy green foliage and fragrant white blossoms that are followed by the fruit. Citrus plants need attention to protect them from severe cold, sun scorch, aphids, spider mites, and scale. Grow in full sun; use well-drained soils. Feed regularly with water-soluble fertilizers and watch for the yellowing of leaves that can signal iron deficiency.

Convolvulus sabatius, ground morning glory. We grow it as a trailing perennial to use in hanging baskets and for summer accents in free-standing containers. The lilac-blue flowers close during the day, but the attractive oval foliage takes up the slack. The plants begin flowering while small and continue until fall frost. Grows to a height of 6–8 inches and spreads, with stems that may twine a bit by the end of the summer. Leaf miners may cause damage, and plants can rot if kept too moist. Set containers in full sun or where they will receive afternoon shade. Fertilize regularly with water-soluble plant food.

Dendranthema x *grandiflorum,* florist's chrysanthemum. (Hold the phone: Garden chrysanthemums may soon be switched back to the genus *Chrysanthemum*!) Although technically fall-blooming perennials, you can expect some spring bloom from rooted cuttings set in containers in the spring. The dense, dark green foliage looks good all year if plants are fertilized regularly. The many colors and blossom forms available in chrysanthemums allow all sorts of combinations for fall and early winter color. For best fall bloom, pinch out new growth until July 15. Discontinue fertilizing when the flower buds show color. Plant in full sun, using a well-drained container mix. Watch for aphids, thrips, lacebugs, and caterpillars.

Dianthus sp., dianthus or pinks. All species are cool-weather flowers that dislike heat or severe cold. Some of the species are annuals, others are perennial, and some are fragrant. Plant in the fall to have good-sized plants and abundant flowers in the spring. The many cultivars of dianthus have colors mostly in the pink to crimson range, with a few lavender and white kinds. Certain of the perennials have attractive blue-green foliage in tight mounds. The small plants of pinks combine well with other cool-season kinds and require little care.

Evolvulus pilosus 'Blue Daze'. One of the workhorse container plants, 'Blue Daze' and newer cultivars of this species are staples for hanging baskets and free-standing containers. We grow it as an annual for summer color and find it very heat- and drought-tolerant once established. It has small, oval, blue-green leaves, and small blue flowers on plants that grow to a height of 1 foot and a width of 3 feet. Its plants can't stand dense shade or too much water.

Hamelia patens, firebush. We grow this frost-tender tropical shrub as an annual. In containers it grows to a height and width of 2 feet. It has large, coppery-red leaves and tight clusters of tubular red flowers that attract hummingbirds. It makes an outstanding specimen plant for summer color but can overgrow a container if not pruned periodically. Grow in full sun, in a well-drained container mix. Makes an excellent low-water-use plant once established.

Heteroptyris glabra, red wing. A strikingly different climbing vine that can be perennial if winters are mild. Deciduous. The yellow flowers are followed by winged seeds called samaras; together they create a very unusual visual effect. Somewhat similar in appearance to butterfly vine (*Mascagnia macroptera*). A plant may remain shrubby or begin climbing like a vine, depending on its condition and the particular season. Whichever form it assumes, it makes an eye-catching specimen plant for summer color. Grow in full sun.

Hibiscus rosa-sinensis, Chinese or tropical hibiscus. Upright, tree-form plant, with large, flaring, 6-inch blossoms in a great range of colors. The flowers last only a day but are quickly replaced, giving a continuous show of summer color. Plants begin blooming when only 2 or 3 feet in height but through the use of plant hormones can be tricked into blooming while quite small. Usually grown with a billowy plant to hide the bare, lower part of the trunk. Grow with afternoon shade during extremely hot weather and prune to maintain the desired shape. Hibiscuses have few problems except for aphids and their rapid growth, which requires yearly shifting up to larger containers. Feed and water regularly. Flowers are visited by hummingbirds.

Jasminum sambac, Arabian jasmine. A shrubby, frost-tender species with large, shining green leaves and highly fragrant white flowers. 'Grand Duke of Tuscany' has double flowers with densely packed petals. We use jasmines as attention-getting accent plants for summer color in large containers. Some Eastern cultures use this jasmine in religious ceremonies. May stop flowering temporarily during periods of intense heat. Water and fertilize regularly with water-soluble fertilizers; grow in either full or part sun. Pinch the tips of branches that try to turn into runners.

Lantana montevidensis, trailing lantana. One of the best plants for all-summer color where water is scarce or expensive. Plant in large containers as it forms dense mounds of stems and small leaves up to 2 or 3 feet high and 6 feet wide. Will sometimes live through mild winters with mulching but we start over each year with new plants. Grow in full sun in a well-drained container mix. It is heat-resistant and has few problems except lantana lacebugs. The strong-smelling foliage is repellent to some people. This one doesn't set lots of unsightly black seeds like the bush lantanas. Needs regular fertilizing, and watering every few days notwithstanding its resistance to heat and dryness.

Petunia x *hybrida,* petunia. Virtually all varieties of petunias burn out or stop blooming during our summer heat, so we grow them as spring-blooming annuals. We set them in containers or hanging baskets early in the spring and protect them if heavy frost is predicted. Many colors and blossom sizes are available, some of which trail attractively. Feed petunias regularly, and watch out for cutworms and caterpillars. The variety 'Summer Madness' tolerates our heat better than most.

Mandevilla x *amoena* 'Alice du Pont', mandevilla. In the ground, this tropical, twining vine could reach 20–30 feet in height but rarely exceeds 8 feet in containers. It produces large, oval, rough-textured leaves and clusters of deep pink, scentless flowers from summer until fall frost. It makes a very showy plant and is especially effective when trained up a sturdy, tall post alongside a plant of allamanda. Stays in flower longer if given afternoon shade. Few problems except spider mites that can come if plants are stressed. Fertilize and water regularly.

Pelargonium x *hortorum,* geranium. Due to our summer heat, we treat garden geraniums as a cool-season plant for spring and fall color. Available in a multitude of colors including but not limited to shades of crimson, scarlet-red, orange, salmon, pink, rose, purple, white, and shades in between. Grow geraniums in full sun in containers of well-drained soil. The ivy-leafed types trail nicely in hanging baskets, and the "zonal" types grow upright. Fertilize regularly and pinch off spent flowers to extend the flowering season. Extreme cold will kill geraniums. In our container plantings, some cultivars are more heat-resistant than others.

Plumbago auriculata, plumbago or cape plumbago. Plumbago winterkills in our garden, so we grow it as an annual. It forms rather asymmetrical, upright bushes with wandering stems that need occasional pinching of tips or shearing. It is a dependable source of summer color, with sky blue, deep blue, or white flowers from spring through frost. Grow in full to partial sun in well-drained soil. Whiteflies can be a problem.

Portulaca grandiflora, moss rose. This low-growing annual is drought-resistant. It has succulent stems and leaves, and flowers like miniature roses in summer. We also plant its close kin, purslane, whose flowers stay open longer during the day. It has larger, thicker leaves than moss rose. The colors of both are clear and vibrant, and the plants display well when mixed with other flowers in hanging baskets and pots. In mixed plantings, the habit of the blossoms closing during afternoon heat is not so noticeable. Feed and water less frequently than with leafier plants and watch out for snails and slugs.

Asparagus densiflorus (Sprengeri group), asparagus fern. This dense, medium-green plant with needlelike leaves and small white flowers on sprawling branches is a staple foliage plant for hanging baskets and for billowing over the rims of large pots. Small red berries late in the season add to its attractiveness. Branches can be cut from mature plants for use in flower arrangements. This plant will continue to grow well despite being pot-bound. A tender perennial, it can be overwintered with protection. Give it afternoon shade during very hot weather and fertilize regularly.

Rosmarinus officinalis, rosemary. A perennial herb that comes in either creeping or upright forms. Has fragrant, semi-evergreen foliage and attractive lavender-pink or blue flowers. Its leaves resemble pine needles. Creeping rosemary such as the 'Prostratus' cultivar looks good in hanging baskets and the erect forms such as 'Arp' can serve as centerpieces in large containers. Likes well-drained, slightly alkaline soil. Grow in full sun. Severe cold can damage plants, especially if it follows a warm spell during the winter. Rosemary is fairly drought-resistant.

Solanum sp., potato vine. We grow this vigorous, fast-growing vine as an annual, from either tubers or vegetative divisions. It can dominate even a large container if not kept in bounds by pruning. Several cultivars are available in a range of foliage colors, from purple to chartreuse to variegated types. Set the container next to a strong post or tall trellis. White blossoms may come late in the season. Grow in full or partial sun. Feed occasionally and water often. Whiteflies may prove a problem.

Tecoma stans, goldenbells. Upright, bushy plants, 4–6 feet in height, are covered with yellow, trumpet-shaped flowers from summer through fall. Since it seldom lives through our winters, we grow it as an annual. It makes a great upright plant for the center of large containers. Grow in a well-drained container mix, in full sun. It is tolerant to both heat and drought, and resents overwatering.

Tradescantia pallida, purple heart. Trailing perennial with deep purple foliage and succulent stems that produce small, light purple flowers. Use as a flowering and foliage accent plant in containers or hanging baskets. The plants are aggressive and can become invasive, but can be kept in bounds by pruning and training. Grow in full to partial sun. Fairly drought-resistant but looks better if fed and watered regularly. Freezes to the ground during winter but will usually regrow in the spring.

Viola wittrockiana, pansy. One of the few flowers that will give us color through the winter and into spring. A small, low-growing plant that comes in many flower colors and patterns, and in various sizes of blossoms. Pansies display well in basins planted either with a single variety or with an edging of a complementary color. Grow in full sun, in a well-drained container mix. Fertilize regularly, as winter rains leach away plant nutrients. Aphids and fungal rot in wet soil can be troublesome.

Disney's Horticulture, Walt Disney World, Inc.

My admiration for the various Disney enterprises dates back to the founding of Disneyland in Southern California. I was given a behind-the-scenes tour of the operation and was blown away by its complexity and magnitude. Much later, I was one of the American Horticulture Society's Great American Gardeners lecturers at EPCOT and was again treated to a fabulous tour of the several theme centers operated by Walt Disney World Resort. While there, I spent time with Heather Will-Browne, who is with Disney's Horticulture unit. We hit it off famously, with each of us recognizing that we had found a fellow "plant nut." Heather submitted this list of plants that grow well in containers at the various Disney enterprises around Lake Buena Vista, Florida:

Begonia 'Dragon Wing'. This is absolutely my favorite container plant, particularly for growing by itself as a specimen plant. It grows into a large, vigorous plant. Although it has a rather upright habit, its long branches loaded with blossoms tend to descend, giving it a weeping appearance. I have found it to be hungry for plant food; it develops the best color when fertilized on a regular basis. It doesn't seem to be bothered by pests, either. What a great plant!

Caladiums. The many color variegations in

caladiums are fantastic in containers during our summer months. We site them where they can receive moderate shade throughout the day. Caladiums require no special care, and the colorful foliage lightens up even the darkest corners. We use many cultivars. My personal favorite is 'Pink Symphony', but one of the newer cultivars, 'Florida Sweetheart', attracts a lot of favorable comment.

Canna 'Tropical Rose'. We plant a lot of this cultivar in containers, not only for its upright plant habit but also for its compact growth, topping off at about 3 feet. The flowers of 'Tropical Rose' are full and well-rounded, and have a very pretty rose color that is compatible with many other flowers.

Orthosiphon stamineus, cat's whiskers, is an attractive, erect, dark green plant with large, wispy spikes of lavender or white flowers. Best planted in a large container, in full sun or partial shade.

Coleus 'Mars'. This is one of the sun-tolerant coleus cultivars, which we grow in light shade all day or afternoon shade to reduce heat stress. This one has small, multicolored leaves and a dense plant habit. It makes a great filler plant that doesn't seem to mind a bit of crowding in containers.

Scaevola, fan flower, 'New Wonder', has a dense, spreading habit of growth. It is continually covered with blooms during the summer months. It's a great plant for accenting yellow and pink flowers grown with it in containers or hanging baskets. Grow in full sun. Not much maintenance is required other than regular feeding and watering.

Gaura 'Whirling Butterflies' and 'Siskiyou Pink'. Both of these send up numerous slender stems that are soon covered with 1-inch diameter blossoms that dance in the slightest breeze. The plants look airy but expand rather rapidly and need to be centered in large containers for height. They can be used alone or in combination with other airy-looking plants.

Impatiens. We have tried many color series of impatiens. Colors chosen from the 'Accent' or 'Super Elfin' series are excellent performers in our climate. Either series offers a tremendous range of colors and maintains a nice growth habit.

Impatiens 'Fiesta' series. These have double flowers with blossoms composed of more than one layer of petals, like miniature roses. The 'Fiesta' series are extremely free-flowering and are the most floriferous double impatiens I've ever seen.

Ipomoea, ornamental sweet potato, 'Blackie' and 'Marguerita' complement each other with their dramatic chocolate-purple and chartreuse foliage colors. We use them primarily to cascade from pots and hanging baskets, but when pruned back they can also make a dense filler plant.

Lantana 'Gold Mound'. When we plant this one in a sizeable pot and give it a few weeks to grow, it can be counted on to fill the pot and billow over the rim. It has a dense habit of growth and makes a good filler plant for combining with other robust species of flowers and foliage plants.

Lyricashower 'Blue' and 'Rose' (*Calibrachoa*) have performed extremely well in our environment. They are low-growing and work best as a cascading plant in a container or hanging basket. They are sensitive to day length and will not bloom during the short days of winter. Expect the best show of blooms in spring and early summer. Little maintenance is required. *Lyricashower* and Million Bells have genes from the same species.

Petunia 'Wave'. The colors in the 'Wave' series

cascade like crazy. They are continually in bloom. In our Central Florida climate their optimum show of color is spring and early summer. Except for regular feeding and watering, a minimal amount of maintenance is required.

Torenia 'Summer Wave Blue' works well as a trailing filler flower in containers. Its pretty blue flower color really sets off other colors. The only problem with this variety is its dense, vigorous habit of growth. You may have to cut it back to keep it from crowding other flowers grown with it.

Verbena 'Tapien' color series can be used as a filler and trailing plant with about any combination of flowers or foliage plants. Its lacy leaves and long branches weave among other flowers planted with it.

Heather added, "I work with containers of flowers nearly every day, and have some favorite combinations. At the top of my list are purple coneflower (*Echinacea*) 'Magnus' and globe amaranth (*Gomphrena*) 'Strawberry Fields', grown together."

Riverbanks Zoo and Botanical Garden, Columbia, South Carolina

Atop a steep, rocky bluff where the Broad and Saluda Rivers meet to form the Congaree stands the Riverbanks Botanical Garden. You pass through the zoo to reach it. Jenks Farmer, curator of the Botanical Garden, sent a list of some of the best container plants they've tried

at Riverbanks. He added, "Any plant that is listed as seasonal may be a true perennial, but in our climate is used only for one season of display."

Seasonal Container Plants for Summer Interest

Alocasia odora, giant elephant ears. Massive, upright, acid green, with arrowhead-shaped leaves. Perennial.

Argyreia nervosa, woolly morning glory. Dramatic, heart-shaped, velvety leaves on a vine that climbs to 15 feet. Lavender flowers. Summer seasonal.

Clerodendrum myricoides 'Ugandense', butterfly flower. Pale blue flowers on large, open plants that mingle well with other plants. Perennial.

Crinum augustum 'Erythrophyllus', purple crinum. Dramatic, deep burgundy, upright foliage and spidery white flowers. Summer seasonal.

Cycas taitungensis, emperor sago. Bold form and dark green leaves. Short, woody trunk.

Lantana camara 'Fuchsia', shrub verbena. Reliable, all-summer color, hot orange flowers. Perennial.

Ruellia brittoniana, Mexican petunia. Reliable, dark purple flowers on slender but erect stems. Perennial.

Solanum seaforthianum, St. Vincent lilac. Blue to lavender flowers followed by loads of bright red fruit. Summer seasonal.

Tibouchina urvilleana, princess flower. Reliable, large, velvety purple flowers. Tall, open plant. Perennial.

Tradescantia 'Burgundy Centaur', spiderwort. Rich burgundy leaves and stems on a trailing, tough-as-nails plant. Summer seasonal.

Container Plants for Winter Interest

Brassica juncea var. *rugosa,* purple leaf mustard. Burgundy-colored, quilted leaves. Damaged by the coldest nights. Winter seasonal.

Brassica oleracea 'Lacinato', dinosaur kale. Blue-gray leaves with very puckered texture. Never damaged by frost here in winter. Winter seasonal.

Brassica 'Red Bor', purple kale. The deepest burgundy leaf of any winter kale. Winter seasonal.

Cupressus arizonica var. *glabra* 'Carolina Sapphire'. Used as an economical, instant centerpiece for winter containers. Silvery foliage. Cold-hardy, woody shrub.

Erysimum perofskianum 'Gold Shot'. Fresh green foliage all winter, with sporadic flushes of fragrant, yellow flowers. Winter seasonal.

Nemophila maculata 'Penny', five spot. Reliable, low-growing, with succulent, trailing foliage and near-black flowers all winter. Annual.

Petroselinum crispum 'Gigante D'Italia', Italian heirloom parsley. Rich green, dissected leaves that are never hurt by frost. Biennial, grown as a winter-spring annual.

Cleveland Botanical Garden, Cleveland, Ohio

In past years, I have lectured at this botanical garden when it was known as the Garden Center of Greater Cleveland. Along with the name change have come many improvements in facilities and services to meet the needs of this great metropolitan area. Cleveland fronts on Lake Erie, which not only puts it into the snow belt but also tends to moderate the summer heat. Much of the city is in hardiness zone 5, but nearby highlands fall into zone 4.

Paul J. Pfeifer, horticulturist at the garden, wrote, "Attached is a list of plants we grew in our terrace containers this past summer. All the containers were located in full sun, and all performed beautifully. Many visitors commented that it was our nicest container plant display in years. We used ten to twelve different plants in each container, and although I was a bit nervous that the effect would be too busy and wild, the plantings were quite beautiful and spectacular. Our goal was to create 'show-stopping' container plantings and, based on comments from visitors, I think we succeeded.

Among our best performers were:

Abutilon pictum 'Thompsonii' (flowering maple, mottled foliage)

Beta vulgaris var. *flavescens* 'Bright Lights' (Swiss chard, mixed colors)

Buddleia davidii 'Honeycomb' (yellow butterfly bush)

Brugmansia and *Datura* cultivars (angel's trumpet)

Gomphrena globosa 'Woodcreek Red' (globe amaranth)

Helichrysum bracteatum 'Golden Beauty' (dwarf strawflower)

Helichrysum petiolare 'Green Gold' (variegated false licorice)

H. petiolare 'Lemon Yellow' (yellow false licorice)

Heliotropium arborescens 'Marine' (heliotrope)

Ipomoea batatas 'Blackie' (sweet potato vine, dark purple)

I. batatas 'Marguerita' (sweet potato vine, chartreuse)

Lantana camara 'New Gold' (yellow lantana)

Miscanthus sinensis 'Gracillimus' (white-stripe eulalia grass)

Panicum virgatum 'Heavy Metal' (variegated switch grass)

Petunia axillaris 'Blue Surfinia'

P. axillaris 'Venice Blue' (one of the 'Supertunia' colors)

Solanum jasminoides 'Variegata' (variegated potato vine)

Zinnia 'Sun Gold'

Appendix

A Short List of Mail-Order Sources of Seeds or Plants Suitable for Containers

W. Atlee Burpee & Co., Warminster, PA 18974. Old mail-order seed company offering modern as well as heirloom varieties.

Casa Flora, Inc., P.O. Box 4110, Dallas, TX 75241. Casa Flora is *not* a mail-order company but they specialize in ferns, and you will see their tags in southern garden centers. They are a good source of information if you are writing about ferns for a newsletter or in a newspaper column.

ForestFarm, 990 Tetherow Road, Williams, OR 97544-9599. This nursery offers an amazing variety of woody and herbaceous cultivars. Write for price of their catalog.

Heronswood Nursery, 7530 288th St. NE, Kingston, WA 98346, (206) 297-4172. Mail-order source of plants of rare and unusual species and cultivars. Write for price of catalog.

Logee's Greenhouses, 141 North St., Danielson, CT 06239. A good source of rare plants, many of them tender species for greenhouse culture in the North. Write for price of catalog.

Park Seed, 1 Parkton Ave., Greenwood, SC 29647-6002, (864) 223-7333. Leading mail-order seed source. Container varieties are not listed separately but the descriptive copy covers adaptability to containers.

Plant Delights Nursery, Inc., 9241 Sauls Road, Raleigh, NC 27603, (919) 772-4794. Write for price of their catalog of hostas and other shade-tolerant plants.

Richter's Herbs, 357 Highway 47, Goodwood, Ontario, Canada L0C 1A0. Unusual herb seeds and plants. Write for price of catalog.

Stokes Tropicals, P.O. Box 9868, New Iberia, LA 70562. Source for hard-to-find ginger lilies, elephant ears, ornamental and fruiting bananas, etc. Write for price of catalog.

Thompson & Morgan, Inc., P.O. Box 1308, Jackson, NJ 08527-0308. Very wide assortment of seeds of hard-to-find species and varieties.

Andre Viette Farm and Nursery, P.O. Box 1109, Fisherville, VA 22939. Extensive assortment of perennials. Write for price of catalog.

Reference Books For Learning More About Plants for Containers

Only the most modern plant encyclopedias and catalogs mention the adaptability of plants to container growing. I found these useful when writing this book, and I am grateful for their insights. Unfortunately, no comprehensive book on annuals has been published in the U.S. recently, and in existing books on annuals little mention is made of adaptability to growing in containers.

The Southern Living Garden Book, edited by Steve Bender, and published by Oxmoor House.

Gardening by Mail: A Source Book, edited by Barbara J. Barton, published by Mariner Books. Look here for addresses of mail-order sources of seeds, plants, and bulbs, and garden supplies. Named a "Great American Garden Book" by the American Horticultural Society.

Hardy Herbaceous Perennials, by Jellito and Schact, published by Timber Press.

Hortus Third, published by Macmillan. Incomplete and outdated but still useful for looking up obscure species, botanical, and common names. I understand that an updated reprint is not forthcoming.

Index of Garden Plants: The New Royal Horticultural Society Dictionary, by Mark Phillips. I use this modern reference now in place of *Hortus Third,* especially for up-to-date botanical names.

New Varieties to Know and Grow, by Sara Rowekamp, Oak Leaf Publications, P.O. Box 58649, Cincinnati, OH 45258. This book is scheduled to be updated yearly. It includes new varieties for garden use as well as containers.

The Sunset National Garden Book, published by Sunset Books, Menlo Park, CA

Plant Performance Trials Open to the Public

Virtually all major botanical gardens and the horticulture departments of some land-grant universities have summer displays of new flower cultivars and varieties. But an equally good place to learn about new and coming plant developments is at any of the Trial Grounds of major garden seed producers and marketers. These have decreased in number during the past few years due to consolidation within the garden seed industry, but the survivors have increased the size of their trials and have expanded them to include trials of flowers in containers. Take your camera and visit:

Ball Horticultural, Town Road, West Chicago, IL. Ball is a long-established horticultural conglomerate that owns several garden seed or plant companies. Their performance trial rows and special container trials are outstanding. The best time to see them is usually the first or second week in August, but prime time can vary from year to year. Phone ahead for information, (630) 231-3500.

Goldsmith Seeds, Inc., Hecker Pass Road, Gilroy, CA. The staff at Goldsmith stages a brilliant show of performance trials of seed-grown flowers, including previews of coming attractions, in late July and early August. The equable climate of Northern California enhances the color of flowers, creating innumerable photo ops. For information, phone (408) 847-7333.

Johnny's Selected Seeds, Foss Hill Road, Albion, ME. For New England, there's no better place to see new varieties than these trials. Mid-August is the best time to visit. Phone ahead for directions, (207) 437-9294.

Park Seed, Cokesbury Road, Greenwood, SC. These trials are open to the public from dawn to dark for much of the summer. The best time to visit is during the Flower Festival held the third week in June. Come early in the morning or late in the day to minimize the impact of the heat. No need to phone; highway signs in Greenwood point the way.

Proven Winners. Many producers and marketers are involved in the Proven Winners network, but most are strictly wholesale. I know of one retailer who grows all the new and coming winners, and who has been very helpful to me in arranging photos: Weidner's Gardens and Greenhouses, Encinitas, CA. Phone ahead, (760) 436-5326.

Stokes Seeds, St. Catherines, Ontario, Canada. Just a short drive beyond Buffalo, New York, Stokes operates a small but well-run trial grounds that benefits from the lake effect in climate. Their mail-order seed business also has a U.S. office, but the flower and vegetable trials are at their Canadian headquarters. Late July and early August is the best time to visit.

Acknowledgments

The author would like to thank several companies and individuals who provided photo ops for this book:

Ball Horticultural Company, West Chicago, for arranging what had to be the most extensive demonstration of planted containers ever staged anywhere

Cole and Company, Marietta, Georgia, for staging photos of hypertufa containers, planted or awaiting custom assortments of plants for upscale landscapes

The horticulturists at the garden center at Craven Pottery, Commerce, Georgia, for showing how to use very large containers in landscaping a shopping center

Fafard, Inc., Anderson, South Carolina, for technical information on premium-grade potting soils and container mixes

The horticultural staff at Fearrington Resort, Pittsboro, North Carolina, for imaginative combinations of the latest in flowers for containers

Steven R. Hill, Ph.D., botanist with the Illinois Natural History Survey

Dan Hinkley of Heronswood Nursery, Kingston, Washington, for arranging for me to photograph containers in his landscape of rare or unusual plants

The Ken Loader family of Gethsemane Gardens at Sumner (near Christchurch), New Zealand, for showing me how hypertufa containers are used for growing N.Z. native plants

MacDonalds Nursery, Virginia Beach, Virginia, for imaginative combinations of heat-resistant flowers in containers

Megan Meyer of Gardens Through the Seasons, Penfield, New York, for information on making ultralightweight hypertufa basins

Joann Viera of Tower Hill Botanic Garden, Boylston, Massachusetts, for demonstrating container plantings for short-season areas

Katie Moss Warner and the horticultural staff at Walt Disney World Resort for showing me their landscaping when I lectured at the 1999 EPCOT International Flower and Garden Festival at Lake Buena Vista, Florida

Westmoor Country Club, Milwaukee, Wisconsin, for allowing me to photograph large containers around their clubhouse.

Evelyn and Mary Weidner of Weidner's Greenhouses, Encinitas, California, who had several containers designed and planted for my visit there in 1998

Without the help of friends, I would not have been able to introduce you to the art and technique of making and planting hypertufa troughs, sinks, pots, and tubs. To name a few:

Don and Bev Sudbury of Salt Lake City, Utah, have a garden full of outstanding hypertufa troughs of various sizes and designs, planted with lovely, rare alpine species. Don makes the troughs and Bev plants them, and they both enjoy teaching others how it is done. I was fortunate to have been invited to stay with the Sudburys while Don was taking a class of Utah Master Gardeners through the steps of making forms, mixing mortar, and shaping troughs.

And I was invited to come to the Atlanta suburb of Stone Mountain, Georgia, to meet Mary Braswell. A few years ago, Mary began making and selling troughs, pots, and garden decorations of hypertufa throughout the Southeast, through her business called English Garden Troughs. She took me all around the Atlanta area to show me how designers are using her creations in landscapes, and showed me that she uses sand instead of Perlite in her troughs to give them a rustic look.

Up in Greensboro, North Carolina, Janice Nicholson showed me the artistic pieces she shapes from hypertufa to sell through her garden center, Gethsemane Gardens. On opposite sides of the world I saw in the Royal Botanical Gardens, Edinburgh, Scotland, the original livestock watering troughs that inspired the first hypertufa copies, and all around New Zealand, hypertufa troughs planted with their native alpine species. How does that old Beatles song go? "I'll get by, with a little help from my friends!

Mary Braswell of English Trough Gardens, Stone Mountain, Georgia, for adding greatly to my information about and enthusiasm for hypertufa containers, and for introducing me to landscape designers who are featuring them in upscale landscapes.

Don and Bev Sudbury of Salt Lake City, Utah, for enrolling me in their Master Gardening class on making hypertufa containers and showing me how they use them to grow rare Rocky Mountain alpine flowers.

Index